JANET O. HAGBERG
ROBERT A. GUELICH

Stages in the Life of Faith

The Critical Journey

Sheffield Publishing Company

Salem, Wisconsin

For information about this book, contact:
Sheffield Publishing Company
P.O. Box 359
Salem, Wisconsin 53168
Phone: (262) 843-2281
Fax: (262) 843-3683
e-mail: info@spcbooks.com

To Bill and Joyce

Our Companions
on the Critical Journey

Contents

Preface

The Critical Journey has emerged much to our surprise and contrary to our "best laid plans." We did not set out to write a book together. We did not intend to do any more than explore together experiences in the journey of faith. We each had other writing projects and commitments, Janet in the world of corporate management with her background in educational psychology and Bob as the Teaching Minister of Colonial Church with his background in New Testament studies.

Janet was set to write a book on leadership as a sequel to her work, *Real Power*, which had explored the use of power in corporate structures. She had even started her research for a book that would further enhance her standing and credibility in the corporate circles and bring her more work as a consultant. Instead she was steadily drawn to write this book on the spiritual journey—hardly a popular topic and certainly unlikely to be a consulting topic in the corporate world!

It all began when Bob heard Janet speak in a leadership seminar about the use of power in personal relationships. Seeing a correlation between how we relate to each other and how we relate to God, he asked her to consider doing a seminar on that theme for Colonial Church. Janet consented but only on the condition that the two of them jointly prepare the seminar, which would focus on the stages of faith. Five months later, they held their first seminar, The Journey of Faith. *The Critical Journey* began to grow out of that seminar.

Now a few years later, a friend has put it together for Janet by observing: "Perhaps this *is* the book about leadership." Perhaps it is. Janet believes that unless we closely attend to the spiritual undergirding of our lives, our leadership development can become rigid or even atrophy. By contrast, if we nurture our spiritual life and experience the healing of life's wounds, especially after age thirty-five, new levels of intuitive, inspired, courageous, and creative leadership will emerge that are unique to our own life's calling.

At the time this project began, Bob had recently joined the staff of the Colonial Church of Edina, Minnesota, as the teaching minister responsible for the adult education program. Having spent his previous career in New Testament studies as a seminary professor, he was becoming more sensitive to the life of faith as reflected in the joys and struggles of the laity. He also was aware of how little the more technical theological jargon and even the "church"-talk communicated to the laity. For this reason, he felt that Janet, a lay person exploring her own journey of faith, would be a good colleague to help others recognize and identify their journey.

Bob was also continuing to write more technically in the field of New Testament studies. His call to Colonial Church included the dual task as theologian-in-residence, which gave him two days each week to continue his work on a commentary on Mark's Gospel for the Word Bible Commentary Series. Three years behind schedule at the time, he had refused all writing requests except those directly aligned with the work on Mark. He certainly had not considered writing a book on spirituality for the laity. Hardly a specialist in "spirituality," he had not even attempted to write for the laity.

Neither of us was ready for this book. Yet in another way we both were ready. It has come at the intersection of our experiences and thinking, the crossroads where spirituality meets the world, where the sacred and the secular intersect. Both of us have greatly benefited from the intersection.

So we write, not knowing where this book will lead us but knowing that we have needed to write it. We know that our own spiritual journeys are part of our inner call to write once again— Janet with her fountain pen and Bob with his computer. And we have both grown immensely from this call. Each of us has helped the other to keep the tension alive between the secular and religious perspectives in order to discover that which was ultimately spiritual. This has been our greatest challenge.

We recognize that more academic approaches to the stages of faith have preceded. Many approaches have been based on extensive research. Even other more popular treatments of the phases of one's faith journey have appeared. Some readers have found these "stage" approaches helpful; others have found them too limiting. Ours is simply an attempt to provide another guidebook for the reader to use to help identify some of the mileposts on the journey of faith. We trust it will do that for you the reader.

We gratefully acknowledge the role that the Colonial Church of Edina, Minnesota, has played in the writing of this work. The staff has encouraged us to teach the Journey of Faith seminar on which *The Critical Journey* has been based and has provided the setting for these seminars. We are especially indebted to the many seminar participants who shared their journeys with us and helped us develop further the contours of the journey. We also thank the readers of the early drafts who gave us valuable comments: Skip Goodmanson, Darlene Stendsby, Robert MacLennan, Jeannette Bakke, Barbara Spradley, Kay Vander Vort, Donna Harling, Miriam and Chet Meyers, and Susan Sands. A special thanks to Knox Coit for his extensive review and especially to Andrew and Nancy Helmick who have lovingly and painstakingly edited our manuscript. We also thank Bonnie England, who has graciously and without one complaint typed, retyped, printed, reprinted, copied, and recopied the typescript. We would be amiss should we fail to acknowledge our spouses to whom we have dedicated this book, Bill Svrluga and Joyce Guelich, whose patience, companionship, and support are very much a part of our journeys! And so . . . on with the Journey.

Janet Hagberg and Robert A. Guelich
Easter, 1989

1995 Preface

Witnessing the republication of *The Critical Journey* is a joyous occasion, yet writing this new Preface is painful for me. The pain stems from the sudden death in 1991 of my soul friend and coauthor of this book, Bob Guelich. He had a heart attack near his island cabin in northern Minnesota at the young age of fifty-two. At the time, I was on a travel study tour of the Soviet Union and Eastern Europe and out of touch until after the funeral was over. I will always remember precisely where I was in Prague when I heard the news. I lay awake all that night weeping, remembering our friendship and feeling sad and forsaken.

Since then, the journey of grief has taken me to places within myself and in the outer world I would never have imagined. As difficult as it has been, I've found the last three years of grieving to be a cleansing and healing time.

To honor Bob I'd like to include a few stories that relate to his life and particularly to our collaboration on *The Critical Journey*. I remember the times that we would both get discouraged while writing this book. These were times when we were waiting for a breakthrough or when something we had written needed to be rewritten. Once, when I came dragging into our weekly meeting, Bob said to me, "Do yourself a favor. Before our next meeting, read the first three chapters of the book. God is in this book, and you'll reexperience that." I went back and read the opening chapters and I was truly rejuvenated.

When we were writing the chapter on stage six, the life of love—which neither of us had experienced as our home stage—we struggled with how to describe it without making it sound too simple or too complex. One conversation we had remains deep in my heart. Bob was captivated with the term "Christ-like" but he thought that many people interpreted the term to mean duplicating Christ's actions. Then he said something like this: "Being Christ-like really means allowing God to do anything God wants in our lives, just as Christ allowed God to do anything in his life." That idea has grown within me as I allowed the truth of it into my consciousness.

Part of my grief process after his death included trying to draw Bob's portrait from a picture I have of him on my desk. I began drawing earnestly, but I soon found this labor of love turning into a frustrating task. I couldn't quite capture his likeness. I tried harder but it just wasn't working. I decided to pray to center myself and to get direction. During my prayer I heard a voice inside me calmly saying, "Stop trying to draw me, Janet. Write for both of us." I was taken aback and wondered if I was imagining things. But I heard it a second time. So I thanked God for the clear message. Prior to this time I had published one book about every four or five years. Within the following year, however, I worked on four writing projects and went on to write two books during the next three years. I feel inspired, energized, and loved. I am writing for both of us.

Because he had a heart condition, Bob never thought he would live to graduate from high school. But his faith allowed him to become comfortable with the finiteness of his life. He told me several times that he was not afraid to die. Maybe that's why he had such a great sense of humor and a taste for the finer things in life—like Ghirardelli chocolate. As a special tribute to both his humor and taste, I go to his graveside regularly and put Ghirardelli chocolate chips on his headstone and eat a few myself.

I've also reflected on how Bob's death has affected my own stage of faith, since he and I regularly asked each other what stage of faith we were experiencing. I know I have visited all six stages again as a result of this experience. I have screamed at God, doubting any meaning in such a loss. I stopped teaching classes on *The Critical Journey* for a few years because the class brought back too many memories of our teaching days together. I have waited expectantly for someone to give me the answers. But while I waited and cried and mourned, I was fortunate to experience a strong loving community around me. And in the midst of it all I felt at times more deeply connected to Bob's spirit than I had felt to the living Bob. In the perspective I have now gained over three years later, I think the most lasting effect his death has had on me has been to help me finally burst through the *Wall* to experience interior freedom for the first time.

I will close this Preface with an observation from Bob himself. He was the Teaching Minister at Colonial Church in Minneapolis before he left to teach at Fuller Seminary. In the fall of 1984 he wrote a column in our weekly newsletter about his vision of adult education at our church. His vision and wisdom are evident in these words.

> Far too often we fail to realize that for the Christian all of life, each day of our life, and each activity within each day becomes a part of the life of faith. We cannot separate life and faith without denying one or the other. But how faith and life interface for the Christian is part of growing in faith. We can learn about Christianity and other religions, we can learn about the Bible and the church, we can learn about ourselves and others without learning to live by faith.
>
> I want our program in adult education with all its variety ultimately to provide those involved a foundation in living the life of faith, in living out what it means to be a Christian in the everyday context of each of us. Do join us in one or more opportunities to make our church a learning community of faith.

Janet O. Hagberg
January 1995

Introduction

The spiritual journey is deceptively simple and at the same time highly complex. Our respect for this journey deepened as we wrote this book. Describing this paradox of spirituality is difficult, and can really only be "lived into." This is why the journey is so profound. And that is why it is critical. It is life itself. *The Critical Journey* is, at its core, a description of the individual's *spiritual journey;* our response to or faith in God with the resulting life changes.

Depending on your starting point, this book addresses one or all of the following issues.

The struggle to find meaning and wholeness. Many people experience a measure of success and satisfaction in their lives or professions. Then over a period of time they slowly become disillusioned with that success. Some begin to wonder if there is not something more, a deeper meaning, for their lives. They seek greater fulfillment, more balance or, perhaps, something beyond themselves. Quite self-sufficient, they often fail to recognize that the struggle may not be simply vocational but, at its core, spiritual. The quest for meaning, balance, and wholeness frequently expresses a need for a relationship with Someone beyond our-selves to give orientation, direction, and meaning to our lives. Pascal described each of us as having a "God-shaped vacuum" within our lives that only God can adequately fill. Yet, for some, traditional religious stereotypes impede rather than enhance such a solution. This book will show that the spiritual journey does not require the stereotypes of religion. It is a deep and satis-fying journey by itself. In fact, we believe that the path to finding meaning ultimately converges with the journey of spirituality.

The crises of values and identity at midlife. Perhaps too much has been written about the midlife crisis. Yet people do continue to be surprised by it and then suffer through it year after year. Many factors precipitate a midlife crisis, and they differ from individual to individual. Frequently, however, a spiritual need provides a key ingredient. Sometimes people lose their faith dur-ing the crisis because they never thought life could be so hard. Their God is too small to cope with the cruel turn of events, or is blamed for causing the pain. Sometimes people caught in midlife crisis turn to God for the first time as they become aware of their inadequacy to handle life alone. Others find that the midlife struggle affords them the opportunity to return to a lapsed or dormant faith—as though returning home from a far country. We have observed that a midlife crisis brings a time of ferment on the critical journey. It is a prime time to consider or reconsider what the spiritual journey really means to you.

Questions about the spiritual journey. Many people have had a simple faith since their childhood. Now, as adults, they begin to reflect more on their faith, wish to grow deeper in their faith, and want to learn how to proceed. At the same time, the return of religious fervor in some segments of our society has raised an-other concern: "How can other people who say they have faith, as I do, be so different from me in the way they believe and act? Am I wrong? Are they deceived? Should I change? Do they have something I don't have?" This concern arises for those within the Church as well as those outside traditional religious circles.

For those seeking to understand, we will provide a descrip-tion of the phases, stages, stopping places, and transition times along the journey of faith—the spiritual journey. This description should help the curious discover where they are now on their journey, as well as appreciate where others are. For those who choose to take the journey, it is lifelong. The longer the journey, the more nuances it takes on and the more it opens us to broader experiences. Yet, a journey must progress step by step. So it is with our spiritual journey.

The quest for self-actualization. A whole subculture of people exists today for whom the quest for self-actualization and wholeness provides their reason for living. Through counseling, education, psychology, psychic awareness, visualization, relaxation, philosophy, fitness, nutrition, and hard work, they strive for new levels of awareness, new and higher levels of consciousness, and ultimately transcendence. They seek to become the most they can be. They are in pursuit of full potential. For some an inner voice begins to ask the central question, "To what end?" Why am I attempting to transcend my humanness? What does it really mean to be human? For these people, *The Critical Journey* can become a guide for the next step, either to begin a very different spiritual journey or to break through the ego barriers to experience a deeper transformation of their lives. Perhaps the whole point of life is the acceptance and love of our own humanness, warts and all.

The healing of early religious experiences. We have met far too many people for whom the mention of spirituality and/or religion brings such painful and sad memories that they cannot consider a journey of faith. They often see themselves as good and principled people. Perhaps they even confess to having faith in God. But they have been so damaged by the Church, whether through religious education, religious peers, family, or minister/priest that they bear heavy, ugly scars. The mention of anything remotely religious or related to the Church brings guilt, shame, anger, embarrassment, fear, or overt hostility. They know that something is lacking in their lives. They may even concede that it is a spiritual hunger, but they do not know how to recover from their early recollections. We hope that *The Critical Journey* will provide an occasion for major healing by pointing out how misunderstandings arise and how being "stuck" in the early phases of faith can cause pain for a long time.

For you to know what to expect and not to expect from this book, a few points need to be clarified before we begin describing the journey itself.

We have two objectives in writing this book. First, we want to aid you in understanding your own faith journey by helping you discover where you may be along the way and recognize where you have been. Second, we want you to appreciate where others are on the critical journey at similar or different stages.

The Critical Journey does not tell you exactly how or when to move along your spiritual journey. It does not offer any formulas for spiritual growth. But it does describe the various phases of our spiritual journey and illustrate how people act and think when in those phases. It also will describe transitions and crises that have caused others either to move or to get stuck at various stages. And we will suggest ways by which you can experience each stage through questions and exercises.

Because both of our faith experiences have deep roots in traditional Protestant Christianity (with several side ventures), we are limiting our descriptions to the Christian experience. We do not mean to imply that other forms of spirituality do not exist. However, we do not feel qualified to speak to those experiences. Many people reading *The Critical Journey* will choose to call the Someone beyond us their Higher Power. We personally believe that the Someone beyond us is God. We do take the Scriptures to be God's revelation to us, so we will draw numerous examples from Scripture to illustrate *The Critical Journey*.

This book is not "theological" in the strict sense. We do not approach the subject from God's standpoint, from the standpoint of what Jesus has done or is doing. Much of Christian faith focuses legitimately on who God is, what God has done, and what that means for us and our world. From the outset we assume that God is a vital force who has made a loving overture to all of us. We believe that God's purpose is to bring us into a personal relationship with God and a healthy, whole relationship with one another in our world. We accept the biblical message that God is equally available, equally loving, and equally forgiving of us at all times. Beyond that, God is imminently patient. But we choose to focus on our response and ensuing relationship to God. This book is about our journey, our ups and downs, our advances and retreats, our movement and our stuckness, our prodigal experiences as well as our self-righteousness, in response to what God is doing in our lives.

All journeys are similar; all journeys are different. It is very easy in a book like this for you to assume your journey is wrong if it does not fit what we describe, or that we are wrong because your journey is different. In a sense, all journeys of faith are similar because we are people who do fairly predictable things. Our early stages on the journey are remarkably similar to others. Our "falling apart" experiences also bear much resemblance to others. At the same time, however, each person's walk is unique, not to be duplicated, because of the particular people and events along the way. Read about the critical journey as a loose guide, a globe rather than a road map, and let the message of the journey soak into your soul. The journey is real. It is yours and God's.

We have become acutely aware that the words *spiritual, religious, faith, journey,* and *God* elicit very different and very strong responses from most people. We are aware that we are on holy ground as we approach these topics. And we have made a special effort to relate the concepts of the faith journey to three different groups: those who do not use those terms at all, but consider themselves spiritual, those whose experience is within the conservative tradition, and those whose experience is in a liberal church tradition. In speaking to a variety of groups, we risk inadvertently alienating each group from time to time. We ask your patience and encourage you to read on and let the ideas themselves, the journey itself, entice you.

Regarding content, we will begin *The Critical Journey* by describing the words and metaphors as we are using them, words like *spiritual, spirituality, faith,* and *journey.* We then describe the stage model and sketch our own journeys (chapters 1 and 2).

Chapters 3–9 will develop each phase or stage of the critical journey including the "Wall" (chapter 7). We then conclude with a short Postscript.

Regarding format, each of the six chapters on the stages of faith begins with several quotes from people describing their faith experiences at that phase in their journeys. Next we describe in global terms the essence of that particular stage, followed by a more detailed description of the characteristics of the stage. We recognize that the stages in our everyday life seem more fuzzy and that there is much overlapping when we are in movement. For that reason, our characterizing may seem somewhat artificial or arbitrary to you. Since of necessity we must describe the stages as clearly separate from one another, we hope your struggle with the categories is not too distracting.

Along with characteristics of the stage, we offer biblical examples intended only to illustrate how this characteristic appears in practice at one point in one's life, not to indicate who is at that stage or to imply necessarily that the person involved characterizes one stage. For example, we could illustrate all the stages from the life of Paul, but we have chosen to use only a small portion of his life as an example of a particular stage. Our view of the use of Scripture itself may tell us something about where we are on the journey. We recognize that some readers may be put off by any use of Scripture, others by too little. We will give examples from our own and others' journeys to help illustrate how the stages function at various times in our lives.

Next we will describe the behaviors that arise when people get stuck or caged at that stage. This is followed by a section describing how people have moved from that stage to the next stage, and the obstacles that need to be overcome in order to move.

The last section on experiencing the stage differs considerably from the rest of the chapter. It is not necessary to read it in order to understand the stage. We include it for people who may want to further their experiential (in contrast to intellectual) understanding of the stage or may want to use the material for experiential retreats or workshops. The sections may aid you in finishing some personal work you have not completed at that stage. They may help you rework or revisit some issues you think need a fresh look. Maybe they will help you more fully to understand someone you know or love who is at a different stage from you or aid you to move more fully into that stage from a transition point in your journey. In a few places we make assumptions that the reader knows how to use a personal journal and is familiar with some deepening prayer experiences and imaging. If these are unfamiliar and unworkable, we recommend that you select another means for experiencing the stage from those suggested.

We conclude each chapter on the stages with a summary of the chapter's content. These summaries offer in shorthand form the characteristics illustrating each stage. You are free to reproduce them.

1

The Critical Journey

SPIRITUALITY

Spirituality may be the most misunderstood and misused term of our time. The word itself evokes a mixed reaction of all sorts of memories, ideas, dreads, and joys. Most people relate in some way to the term. For those in the Church, some take the term for granted, some rigidly define it, and others seldom give it a thought. In broader circles, spirituality has come to mean an urge or power within us that drives us toward meaning for our lives. We are astounded by the number of people in secular settings who are drawn enthusiastically to the concept. Most of the people we have talked to in education, corporate, and non-profit settings make it clear that for them "spirituality" is not to be equated with religion. They are emphatic in not wanting to be identified with the Church or organized religion.

Such a response is not new. Evelyn Underhill, a writer and Christian mystic, wrote in 1922 that soldiers at the front during World War I had an enormous amount of natural religion but at the same time were almost totally alienated from religious institutions. She wrote in *The Life of the Spirit and the Life of Today* that many people feel that a secret or private devotion suffices, although she says history does not prove that position to be fruitful. She says "the next most natural and fruitful movement after such a personal discovery of abiding reality, such a transfiguration of life, is always back towards our fellow men; to learn more from them, to unite with them, to help them;

2

anyhow to reaffirm our solidarity with them." Her comments still obtain.

When pursued it becomes clear that this separation between one's self and the Church usually stems from deep unresolved pain or dissatisfaction rooted in early religious upbringing. Sometimes it arises from a contemporary image of the Church as authoritarian, chauvinistic, hypocritical, or unforgiving in nature. Though thirsting spiritually for a relationship, some find it too threatening or the prospects too unsatisfying to have to return to a painful image or experience associated with God and the religious realm. This group may actually scorn the Church because it is not intellectually acceptable to live with a reality that can only be accepted on faith. "To believe in something nonverifiable," they say, "is to be weak in one's thinking."

A point comes on the spiritual journey, however, when a healing of one's early religious experience must occur in order for wholeness to be realized. This healing requires a transformation of the person *and* of the traditional religious images, symbols, and words. Such transformation allows for a new way to experience these traditions and, therefore, a whole new appreciation of spirituality. It's coming full circle to wholeness. We shall discuss this more in chapters 6–8.

From our perspective in writing *The Critical Journey,* we have chosen to speak of spirituality ultimately as *the way in which we live out our response to God.* Unless we find this personal, transformational meaning in its fullest sense, the struggle for wholeness will remain unresolved. As Augustine put it in the first paragraph of his *Confessions,* "God created us for a relationship with him and our hearts are restless until we find our rest in God."

FAITH

For those on the journey of faith, what do we mean by our use of the word *faith?*

If someone were to ask, "Do you have faith?" you might answer, "Yes," "No," or "It depends." The question assumes we have an idea of what faith is and can have it or not have it. We also speak of having more faith or less faith, of finding or losing our faith. In fact, we often use *faith* as a noun, an object, something that we can get a hold on.

If someone were to ask, "What faith are you?" you might answer, "Protestant," "Catholic," "Jewish," "Christian," or "Muslim." This answer implies a type or set of beliefs that distinguishes one from others. Frequently set by a holy book, authority figures, tradition, and religious practice, faith used this way describes how we live. In such responses, we are using *faith* as an adjective, a description of the principles that we believe and by which we live.

When we speak, however, of the journey of faith, we use *faith* neither as a noun nor an adjective. *Faith* is a verb, action, the dynamic that drives or gives life to the relationship between us and God. Our response called *faith* is the human recognition, on the one hand, that God is God, and, on the other hand, that each of us is special. It is the recognition that we are most fully human when we acknowledge and accept God as God in our lives. As we shall see, we do this in various ways at various stages along the journey. Therefore, *faith* as a verb is neither static, an object to be dissected, nor a qualifier that either puts us on God's side or distinguishes us religiously from one another.

Faith with reference to the journey is simply the process by which we let *God direct our lives* or let God be God. The more we deliberately choose to let God direct our every thought, word, and action, the more profoundly our journey is affected. As we shall note, this journey of faith has various phases or stages. Some find a place along the way where they may stay indefinitely. Some even get stuck at a stage. But we believe that God calls us continually to recognize God's presence in our lives and to respond. And the spiritual or faith journey is first a movement of individual choice toward an acknowledgment of who God is. Further, it is our invitation to God to take control of all aspects of our lives. Once consciously entered upon, this reception of God into our lives effects a continual process of growth rather than a point of arrival.

Not everyone takes this critical journey in the way we are

4

defining it. For whatever reasons, God has no place in their lives. Some have never begun the journey. It holds little interest for them. They have never heard God's call, felt the vacuum in their lives, or reached out to One who stands beyond them. Others appear to have begun the journey and then to have abandoned it, perhaps through disillusionment. This book is not about or for them. This is a book especially for those who want to be or are on the spiritual quest for a greater realization of God in their lives.

JOURNEY

We have selected the analogy of a *journey* to capture the experience of the life of faith. A journey involves process, action, movement, change, experiences, stops and starts, variety, humdrum and surprises. For us a journey implies more than a quick trip from point A to point B. It is more extended, with the time and places between departure and final destination being important for their own sake. Whereas a trip focuses primarily on a destination, a journey has significance when seen as a whole. Journeys are dynamic, not static. There are side trips, returns to former sites, forays into the unknown. A journey cannot be repeated, even if we try. The times and perspectives change the experience. What ideas come to mind when you think of a journey? Here are some of ours:

- a long trip with no strict timetable
- making plans and preparation
- having to pack for a wide variety of experiences
- overpacking for all contingencies
- a map, compass, guidebook
- people to visit along the way
- modes of transportation
- counting the cost in time, energy, and money
- stopping points along the way
- traveling companions

The same words or ideas used to describe real journeys you have taken are useful when considering the faith journey. Many people experience a journey, in contrast to a trip, as undefined with no end in sight. They focus on the process, travel for travel's sake. Others like getting there, accomplishing something. They want to know the shortest and quickest route and have it well marked. Ambiguity bothers them. Delays for sightseeing, rest stops, detours are an aggravation. Some tend to overpack, to bring far more than they would ever need for a real or spiritual journey. Some prefer to travel only with people they know, others are eager to meet new people.

The characteristics that stand out most on vacations and trips in life are generally the qualities that emerge as you proceed along the journey of faith. These qualities are a help and a hindrance. For example, you may be very frustrated to find no clear destination, yet that may be the best learning for you. Or you may want to stop and visit or revisit people from the past whom you have known along the way, but they are unavailable, forcing you to move along. As with any journey, so it is with the faith journey. Our journey of faith connotes *the process and passages in our response to God's overture to us* when we view our lives as wholes.

THE STAGES OF FAITH

We have chosen to use stage theory as the model for our journey of faith. We think of it as one way to illuminate the path of faith, knowing that it is by no means the only way. We believe that mystery occurs all along the journey and that stage theory does not negate that. We understand some people will not be comfortable with the stage approach for various reasons, but we hope they can still derive meaning from the journey descriptions.

The idea of movement through stages or phases within the life of faith has a long history in the Church. Several early leaders spoke of journeys inward and outward. Names of writers and believers like Augustine, Aelred of Rievaulx, Julian of Norwich, John of the Cross, Teresa of Avila, Francis of Assisi, and Ignatius Loyola come readily to mind. In the mid-1800s

Sören Kierkegaard mused on the "stages on life's way." More recently, in the 1920s Evelyn Underhill described stages or phases of faith. Current writers include James Fowler, an academician whose work bridges theology and developmental psychology. His extensive research has focused on seven stages of faith. Gerald Heard reviews various stages of deepening prayer, and Elizabeth O'Connor describes the faith journey. Most recently, Scott Peck, a psychiatrist and psychotherapist, described four stages on the journey in his attempt to integrate psychology and spirituality. It soon becomes apparent that, if not agreement, at least some parallels exist in the description of the direction by many writers/faith seekers on the journey of faith.

What are the stages on the journey of faith? For our purposes we have delineated six.

Stage 1: The Recognition of God

Stage 2: The Life of Discipleship

Stage 3: The Productive Life

Stage 4: The Journey Inward

Stage 5: The Journey Outward

Stage 6: The Life of Love

Some explanations about the stage or phase approach are necessary to answer questions that are sure to arise for you later. Remember that, as with all models used for discussion and understanding, no framework can totally capture a dynamic process.

FLUID AND CUMULATIVE STAGES

The stages on the journey are very fluid. We move back and forth between them regularly, and we can experience more than one stage at the same time. The orderliness of the model (stages 1–6) suggest only the sequence in which we experience the stages as we proceed on the journey. For instance, we do not begin the journey at stage 3. We begin at stage 1. And, though fluid, our journey does not move mysteriously from stage 1 to 6, skipping all the other stages. We may spend years moving back and forth between stages 1, 2, and 3, then in one event, move to stage 4. Then we experience all four stages, for they are cumulative. Each builds on the others preceding it. Depending on your faith history, whether you were raised with no specific faith, agnostic, conservative, evangelical, liberal, or high church, you will experience each stage differently. You may not identify at all with some of the characteristics and identify very strongly with others. We give a wide range of examples in hopes of including most faith journeys.

One of the ongoing problems with sequential models is that higher or later numbers sound better. Consequently, we make the mistake of thinking that people at those stages are somehow better. On the journey of faith, this is not the case. To help explain this, look at our own lives. We experience childhood, adolescence, young adulthood, middle age, older adulthood, and senior citizen status. Each builds developmentally on the previous experience, but we are not inherently better people as adults than we were as children. Perhaps we know more. Certainly, we have suffered more. Perhaps we have used more of our skills and abilities. Certainly we have or have had greater responsibilities. While we always retain childlike qualities, we all expect to become adults and move on through our lives. If we remain children emotionally as we age, there are usually adverse consequences. Yet we needed our childhood as preparation and learning time. Similarly, we view the stages of faith as sequential and cumulative, rather than resulting in the label "better."

HOME STAGE AND REVISITING

Each of us will identify with some characteristic in all the stages at various times in our lives, perhaps even at different times in the week. We do move around from stage to stage—back and forth. The fluidity of the stages comes from the fact that once you have moved to stage 2, for instance, you can move back and forth from 1 to 2 frequently or be at both at the same time. When you have experienced stages 3 and 4, you can move fluidly among all four stages experiencing them simultaneously. And you may bump into the Wall at stage 4 several times before you actually go through it. We submit, however, that each of us has a specific *home* stage (some report two home stages of equal intensity) where we operate most of the time and which best characterizes our life of faith. If you cannot identify a home stage, it may be because you are in a transition from one stage to another. In such case, you do not feel at home in any stage. At the same time, once we have reached stage 3 on your journey as a home stage, for example, you can return to a previous stage because of a critical experience—good or bad. It is common for people to revisit earlier stages from time to time, and to experience them often in a deeper or more personal way than they did the first time. It's like being somewhere for the second or third time, only having more experience now to see the place differently. Experiencing the awe of God for the first time is clearly different than it is years later when you've had a longstanding relationship with God. In that sense the stage model is like a spiral, and we experience more depth each time we recycle through the stages at a higher place on the spiral.

CAGES: GETTING STUCK

Thinking back to the journey analogy, we generally accept that journeys suggest moving, however slowly. We may rest on the way. We may even stop for periods of time to visit friends or sightsee. But we are still traveling. However, we now turn to another experience on the journey that needs to be understood and lived with. We can get stuck along the way; not just visiting people, sightseeing, or pausing to learn but stopping at a stage and getting bogged down in an unhealthy way. It is like getting stuck in the mud, not attempting to resolve the dilemma by getting help but instead just sitting there in the mud.

People usually get stuck at a particular place in the journey because we find it more comfortable to sit than to move. It may be too frightening to move. After a while sitting still moves from comfort to stuckness. When stuck long enough, we get trapped. Frequently, this happens unconsciously. When stuck,

9

we generally do not think we are stuck. To others, however, it is very apparent. The stage has become for us a cage.

When stuck, we are no longer growing in faith. We can become hardened in faith, even a bit crusty. Getting stuck occurs sometimes from our fear of facing the unknown. Other times it results from personal or work crises that we cannot control. Sometimes an illness or death causes us to feel abandoned, thus making us vulnerable to being stuck. Even memories of negative events or relationships, perhaps from our childhood, can surface, and in our fear of facing them, we become stuck. It may even be that we are simply afraid to face the fact that we are loved unconditionally by God. Accepting that means admitting we cannot control God or our destiny. Whatever the cause, becoming caged at a stage is real. If we are aware of it, we will have less likelihood of staying stuck.

We believe there is a natural God-given propensity for us to continue to seek God's will for our lives in ever deepening ways. Being stuck stymies that process at any stage. Sometimes people get stuck early in life and simply stay there. They can be difficult to be around because, unaware of their condition, they have become very defensive about where they are. They too are in God's hands. Having compassion for them and their own journey is the most forgiving response for those who are not stuck. All of us who are or have been caged are getting something from being there. Until we become aware of what we are getting and are willing to give that up or find it some other way along the journey, we will not be able to grow on the journey. If we can see when a stage has become a cage, we can be more understanding of others.

Not all unhealthy, negative, hurtful, selfish, or unconscious behavior means you are stuck. We are imperfect human beings. The whole point of being on a journey is learning to love ourselves with our imperfections because God does. So in each of us, all along the journey, a wide mixture of behavior both wise and unwise, healthy and unhealthy, appears. That is normal. For example, at stage 1 we may look insecure, and at stage 4 we may look selfish; at stage 5 we may look naive, and at stage 3 we may behave overconfidently. These traits are inherent to the stage. But when that behavior begins to dominate or when we become *obsessed* with how we need to behave or how others need to behave, then we have a clear sign that we are becoming caged. Another sign of stuckness is having to be right and convincing others of our rightness, at any stage in our journey of faith. Rightness becomes more important than the journey. Having to be right, whether liberal, New Age, evangelical, or natural is stifling. It keeps us from being open, just as any obsession keeps us from focusing on our own role in a relationship. Noticing our obsessions and righteous attitudes can move us to another place, a different stage, but only if we confront these traits and let them be healed.

By contrast, some people on the journey *appear* to others to be exhibiting strange behavior. They themselves may not even be aware of the fact they are still seeking or even moving. They think they are stuck while in fact they are in a transition. So getting stuck is a complex issue best worked out with a friend or counselor for the journey. We do believe a natural longing exists in most people to seek more and more of the richness and fullness of letting God be God in their lives.

OUTER AND INNER STAGES

In the first three stages, our faith or our spirituality takes its expression most frequently in ways that are prescribed by external standards, whether by the Church, a specific spiritual leader, a book, or a set of principles. Regardless of the standards to which we subscribe, we eventually represent it in our own behavior or try to anyway. Stages 4 through 6 represent a difficult personal transformation and reemerging that require a rediscovery on a different level of what faith and spirituality are all about. These are inner healing stages (spiritually and psychologically) for which the journey cannot be prescribed. We find that everything is interconnected. Since these stages are unique to each person, they defy generalities and make description more difficult. This part of the journey embodies the inner journey to spiritual wholeness.

UNDERSTANDING OTHER STAGES

One of the major reasons for writing this book is to help people become aware of the journey of others and to appreciate those journeys. For that reason we think it necessary to understand the stages other than our own home stage. But this presents us with another difficulty. According to stage theory, we can understand all the stages through which we have been, and we can grasp intellectually the ones immediately ahead of us. But we cannot fully comprehend the actual day-to-day existence of people whose home stage is two stages further along on the journey. We can read the words that describe these people, but living with them, working with them, or being in a meeting with them leaves us perplexed and perhaps frustrated. Returning to our earlier life analogy, it is like teenagers trying to understand what it means to be living in adulthood or middle agers trying to understand the inner life of senior citizens. We have difficulty until we've been there ourselves.

For example, people at the discipleship stage (stage 2), secure with what is right for them and with a strong sense of belonging, may think that people who appear to be questioning or even losing their faith on the journey inward (stage 4) are not strong enough, not faithful enough, not willing enough, or just plain not Christian. Because of their present security in the journey, they find it difficult to comprehend the questioning on the inward journey as another step along the way. When they too fall into the throes of confusion, dissatisfaction, or uncertainty, they may experience other people's questioning of their behavior and only then understand how they were viewing people like themselves earlier. Those on the inward journey (stage 4), on the other hand, can look judgmentally on those people in the discipleship stage (stage 2), who seem to have such ready answers, rather than appreciating them and remembering the times when they too have felt secure. That comes not from misunderstanding stage 2 as much as from the general insecurity of being at stage 4.

We cannot escape most of the crises in our lives, nor should we. In fact, these events frequently provide the energy for movement on our spiritual journey, even when we are stuck along the way. We experience a death of someone close, and we ask questions about our own life. We wonder about meaning. Our present view may become inadequate. We ask deeper questions. Even joyful experiences can propel us forward. We marry someone with a different experience of faith that makes us look again at our own. We have a child and revisit our early faith experiences.

A crisis can knock us off balance, making us afraid, vulnerable, and ripe for change. This also happens in our spiritual journey. We have a crisis in our faith that causes us to reconsider. It might frighten us, at least make us vulnerable. If we become bitter or too resistant, we can get very stuck. But if we let the change or crisis touch us, if we live with it and embrace it as difficult as that is, we are more likely to grow and to move eventually to another stage or spiral in our journey. When we are most vulnerable, we have the best chance to learn and move along the way. In the midst of pain there is promise.

We have already discussed how people can move to earlier stages because of the cumulative nature of the stages. Each one builds on the others, and those we have experienced are readily available to us. Sometimes we revisit them by choice because we have a renewed need for community or because we sense again the awe of God in a deeper way. Other times it seems we are tossed to earlier stages by life events, crises, changes. We know most about moving to earlier stages because they are familiar to us. The more difficult time comes when we feel we are moving to stages beyond our current experience, into the unknown.

It is easy to mislead people into thinking that they can move themselves to the next stage by just doing the things listed, talking to the right people, or setting their mind to it.

Nothing could be further from the truth. The journey of faith is our personal journey, and movement on the journey is the place of mystery, holy ground. Moving from one stage to another reverences timing. It involves bringing our response in sync with God's grace in our lives. God does not make us move. God's grace allows us to move. Consequently, when we describe movement in this book, we are describing how people on the journey have experienced this movement as an example in their lives. Your movements may be similar or different from theirs.

A second consideration in moving to other stages is whether we can make the move alone. Does moving require the help of another? Our observation and experience suggests that it generally does, depending on the stage involved. Each move frequently takes place in conjunction with a faith community, friends, a support group, family, pastor, nun or priest, spiritual director, counselor, or even a therapist. Some of the movements *require* other people, such as moving from stage 1 to stage 2. The very nature of stage 2 is belonging and gaining a group orientation to the life of faith. The move from stage 4 to stage 5 best comes when assisted by someone with a rich spiritual and/or psychological background who can help us work through the Wall. However, the movements between stages 2 and 3, 3 and 4, and 5 and 6, though involving others, can occur without assistance, more self-propelled.

A third consideration about movement between the stages is the consequences. After reading about the stages on the journey, you may find yourself wanting to move because it looks better or will move you further along on the journey. This for many is a natural response, especially at stages 2 and 3. But look at some of the consequences. Moving from one stage to another always causes confusion. We are in a time of limbo between two stages. We may find it exhilarating and exhausting. Nothing seems certain. Something undefined lies ahead. Frequently, the move means loneliness, and can be very upsetting. Moving can inspire love and caring in some. It can also bring fear and mistrust in others. The process means transformation. It always is life changing. Consequently, though the change may be welcomed, it leads over an emotionally rocky road.

Finally, the impetus for movement is frequently an event or experience in our lives over which we have little control. Some mentioned to us are: a health crisis, change in relationships, models of others we want to emulate, a teacher, reaching personal limits, deep questions about oneself, being hurt, responding to others' needs, experiencing God in a new way, telling your own story to another, loss of a relationship, death, developing a quiet time, losing truths once held dear, longing for God. Obviously, one could continue with such a listing. But at that moment in our journey we have a choice. We can choose to plunge ahead not being afraid to be afraid of change, or we can turn back by blocking our feelings and not dealing with the issue. This can be a critical time.

SIMILARITIES AND MOVEMENTS

Strong similarities emerge in certain pairs of stages. In trying to identify where you are personally, you can easily become confused. Therefore, we will attempt to describe some of the major differences that distinguish those stages most easily mistaken for each other.

Stages 1 and 4 are easily confused. The major issue in both stages is self-worth. At stage 1, we struggle with feelings of worthlessness. At stage 4, we struggle with feelings of unworthiness. So when we are at stage 1, we frequently think we are experiencing stage 4. And when at stage 4, we feel like our home stage is stage 1.

Stages 2 and 5 are easily confused. The central issue is letting go. At stage 2, we let go to God for that which we know. At stage 5, we let go to God for that which we do not know (and we live with the ambiguity). Again, while at stage 2, we think we are at stage 5 and vice versa.

Stages 3 and 6 are easily confused. The central issue is giving. At stage 3, we give what we have and can afford. At stage 6, we give what we did not know we had and did not believe we could afford to lose (we lose ourselves). At stage 3, we easily

15

mistake our behavior for stage 6, whereas at stage 6 we do not think about it.

The major movements that we experience along the entire journey are subtle and at times mystifying, because we feel the movements at different levels we are not fully aware of at the time. But a few global movements seem to emerge. We move into forgiveness of ourselves and then from forgiveness to acceptance. From acceptance we move on to unconditional love, both for ourselves and for others. We move from seeing ourselves as the center of the universe to seeing God as the center of the universe from which point we serve others. Another movement involves first learning how to receive from God and others. Then we move to being able to ask God for things, and finally to giving fully to others and to God. Or viewed from another perspective, we move from fear to sureness, to confusion, and then to peace.

These are critical movements, essential to the maturation of our faith. How they are played out in our lives is as varied as our individual natures.

SUMMARY

TERMS

Spirituality —the way in which we live
out our response to God.
Faith —letting God direct our lives (verb).
Journey —an extended trip whose process
is as important as its destination.

Stages on the Journey of Faith

Stage 1: The Recognition of God

Stage 2: The Life of Discipleship

Stage 3: The Productive Life

Stage 4: The Journey Inward
The Wall

Stage 5: The Journey Outward

Stage 6: The Life of Love

Stage Concepts

Fluid and Cumulative Stages

Home Stage and Revisiting

Cages: Getting Stuck

Outer and Inner Stages

Understanding Other Stages

Crisis: A Time for Moving

Similarities and Movements

2

---

*Sharing Our
Faith Journeys*

We all have a choice along the way. We can either be on the critical journey or not. In writing this book, we have clarified for ourselves our own spiritual journeys and have come to a fuller appreciation of our own and others' places on the journey. We have experienced healing. We have come to love the journey. We have become awed by the wonder of it all, the wonder of God's love and grace at work.

Here we will sketch the ups and downs of our own journeys of faith without trying to define, analyze, or defend them. In later chapters, we will elaborate on particular aspects of our journeys. We do this so that you might participate in our journeys. We invite you to reflect on your own journey as you proceed through this book. Your faith experience will no doubt be very different from ours. Surprisingly, ours share several similar points.

JANET'S JOURNEY

My faith journey can be described by the analogy of a roller coaster with numerous ups and downs, some exciting, others scary. It is divided into four main segments summarized by the statement, "My faith has ruined my life." I will explain that later.

Part 1: Early innocence. My early faith experiences just happened. I was raised in a very religious family who tried hard to practice what they preached. We always went to church

(Lutheran) and were an active part of that religious community. I loved singing in choirs, playing piano, listening to "chalk-talks" (talks given while drawing with neon-sensitive chalk), watching missionary slides, and generally being part of the church. I was very involved from an early age. I was "saved" many times during my adolescent years, at church, at camp, and at youth groups.

I experienced a strong sense of belonging in those days, and I learned early to be a leader by getting involved and doing things. I loved school and learning, so I absorbed knowledge like a sponge. My early claim to fame was that I could say the books of the Bible from memory in twenty-five seconds. I also learned hundreds of Bible verses, hymns, and choruses. The most troublesome aspect of those early years was that my church was very strict, conservative, and unbending in its beliefs. There were clear rights and wrongs and strict codes of behavior. The emphasis was on sin and the Cross. That resulted in a heavy sense of guilt and shame.

We were not encouraged to question the beliefs, and that became my dilemma. I remember being concerned about sin in junior high school. One day, after hearing that sin was "anything contrary to the will of God," I asked if God willed for us to fall into big holes. The answer was, "No!" So I asked, "Then why isn't falling into a hole sin?" The answer was an equally firm "God's grace is sufficient." That left me really confused, since I had no idea what "grace" meant.

So I grew up very much belonging, even leading, but at the same time, always wondering about all my myriads of questions. I did not dance, go to movies, or smoke. I even went to a private Christian high school that supported the messages of my church. My mother, however, was the moderating factor in encouraging my growth, my self-esteem, my questioning. My parents showed me by their example what faith was. My early years in faith culminated in membership on a crusade team at age eighteen. Our purpose was to visit other parts of our state, witnessing about our faith by word and song. I had reached the highest pinnacle of my early faith.

Part 2: Faith crisis. I was ripe at that point for something major to happen to my faith. It did. I went to college and all those questions that had been suppressed for years came gushing out. I lost my innocence. My easy faith was gone. I was told Jonah was not really swallowed by the whale. There were contradictions in the Scriptures. Moses did not write the first five books of the Bible. I was ruined! I cried a lot and gained twenty pounds my freshman year. But I learned to love the academic approach to faith. This period of questioning and inner debate was to go on for ten more years. I never left the faith totally (although I called myself an "agnostic"); I just fought with it intellectually.

I became intellectually self-sufficient, rebellious, and intent on my own personal education and growth. And I was truly a product of the times. I was in college and graduate school in the latter half of the 1960s when the "God is dead" idea, as well as Vietnam War protests, were running rampant on the campus. My friends and I spent countless hours discussing whether there was a God, and, if so, what God was doing about war. Another factor in my faith was my marriage (after college) to a Protestant minister's son. We spent most of our early married years rebelling against the church. We rarely made an appearance for ten years (except for an occasional visit to a Unitarian church).

During this period, my fifty-five-year-old mother died suddenly. I was left very alone with my grief and sadness. Although family, friends, and relatives were helpful, I lacked a faith community to help me with the spiritual issues that inevitably arose. I struggled intensely with the meaning of life and death, with values and personal identity. It was a horrible time for me spiritually, so young and so alone.

To find answers, I turned to the world of psychology and social work, the field in which I was working on a master's degree. That led me to an adventure into humanistic psychology, creativity, psychic experiences, Eastern thought, meditation, other levels of consciousness, and New Age awareness. It was a whirlwind period of discovering new ways to be and to think. As part of my training I experienced several forms of counseling.

God worked through those growing experiences, helping me gain mental health. In my career, success was coming my way. I was a college faculty member for several years, then left that to start my own business. All appeared to be under control. I was "making it," and I loved it. Of course, that left me very vulnerable to the unexpected.

Part 3: Life crisis. Right in the middle of my new career development business, a life of travel, and book publishing, the bottom dropped out of my life. The crisis was the failure of our marriage. After ten years of marriage, I was divorced, and I was devastated. I had failed. I remember sitting alone on my sofa for hours, feeling like my entire insides were being scraped away. After months of just muddling through, I began to think there must be something more to base meaning on in life than success. I thought a lot about God and wrote extensively in my journal. I began timidly visiting churches, mostly intellectual ones to avoid a repeat of my youth. I discovered head but little heart. Then I stumbled on a church community that contained heart and head, a community of searchers like myself. The people I met there seemed real, with real questions and real lives and no pat answers.

Gradually, I turned to this community of people who I felt cared for and loved me despite my failure. This, combined with lots of quiet reflection, brought healing. I believe God brought me through that experience partly through the love and caring of that particular faith community. I began to regain my self-esteem and was once again achieving and doing good things in both the wider community and at church. I was back to being successful and being involved. It felt good using the same skills at church I had used successfully in the business world. Once again I had a community of faith and a sense of controlling my life. In retrospect this was a ripe time to be taught yet another lesson.

Part 4: Deepening. I was on a plateau, a very nice plateau. I was sailing along, studying Scripture, consulting and speaking, remarrying, being a stepparent, writing another book. Life was rich. But I was feeling incomplete, a little shallow, too complacent. I wanted to know what was next in my life, what my purpose was, how to somehow deepen my faith. I wanted to grow and did not know how. Independently, three people in my life suggested I talk to a woman they knew who was a spiritual director.

I did not even know what a spiritual director was, but I did go to see her. I entered a program of spiritual direction, foreign to my Protestant tradition, to deepen my faith experience and listen for God's direction for my life. But I, the intellectual, was truly skeptical. Right from the start, I was not at all sure I would like the experience. My spiritual director was Catholic, which for a Lutheran is humbling! And I cringed at the word *direction* (what *leader* wants to be *led?*). Furthermore, she asked for discipline (one hour a day) and used old uncomfortable words like *prayer.*

Now, my faith is ruining my life, as I said at the outset, in the sense that it is changing all my grand designs. I have worked hard all these years, striving to be successful by cultural standards. Now I am finding that success, both in the business world and in the church, while *very* appealing to me, is ultimately not very satisfying. But obedience is. I still respect my work of writing, speaking, and teaching, but I do not think it is the *core* of my existence as much as it used to be.

Deepening my faith meant transforming my life. For me, there was no other choice. As an example of these changes, my life purpose in the first year of spiritual direction was to be a wise leader. In the second year, it was to be wise. Year three was completed with no purpose at all, an experience I now see as an example of the dark night of the soul. In the fourth year, my purpose evolved into just being available. Years five and six and on had the purpose of simply loving. My work has not changed radically. I have changed. The way in which I work has changed too. For a high-achieving, driving personality, this is a profound, ongoing miracle.

I believe spiritual direction to be a lifelong endeavor. Its daily discipline of prayer is teaching me to live more deeply. I am learning to let go, to be led, to forgive, to love, to wait, to serve. I have more peace, more fun, more willingness to deal with anxiety, more willingness to see myself and less fear. I feel spiritual direction and other counseling have led to deep inner healing of pain, both spiritually and emotionally, that I was not even aware of before. It has transformed my early childhood religious misunderstandings into meaningful realities. I don't know where I'm headed in the future, but I'm learning to be more comfortable with that ambiguity. I do know I feel a special, personal connection and love for women who are or have been in prison. I know I love to write, speak publicly, listen to people's stories, and play. I am learning in little bits what love is. And I am open to God's molding me at this point in my life. That for me is a monumental life experience.

BOB'S JOURNEY

My journey falls into three critical periods: precollege, college, postcollege. Charted, it would look very much like an electrocardiogram printout—a continuous wavy line with sudden, arrhythmic spikes up and down.

Part 1: Precollege. I am the oldest of four children in a devout Christian family. When I was hardly a year old, my father left the business world and went into the heart of West Virginia's "billion-dollar coal field" south of Charleston, West Virginia, to begin a work as a Baptist minister. The region had few churches other than the mountain religion or the "holy rollers" with their snake handlers and faith healings. By contrast, my Father's ministry was radical and liberal. Yet by most other standards, I was raised in a very conservative, "Bible believing, Bible preaching" church and home.

Ours was a "conversionist" tradition, one in which a personal conversion was believed to be essential to becoming a Christian. From my earliest memories, I sought and did what was supposedly appropriate to experience that conversion. Responding to numerous invitations to "give my life to Christ," I would be at a loss today to know which one, if not all, of them "worked." Born and raised to live as a Christian should, I never experienced any dramatic conversion experience of lifestyle or feeling. Late in junior high school, after getting into trouble by trying to live by a double standard—one with my unchurched

25

friends and one at home—I again asked God, as best I could at the time, to take control of my life.

Like Janet, I had learned the right answers from early on. Yet my questions were not only allowed but welcomed and answered, since my Father lived and preached a well-articulated, logically consistent message. And the answers always had to be biblical, which meant that I too learned many Bible verses and Bible stories.

At the beginning of high school, my Father accepted a call to a church in South Charleston. It was a move to the big city. There I became very involved as a leader in our church youth group and in a Christian youth organization that included several hundred teenagers from the numerous high schools in the metropolitan area. We had a weekly rally gathering together to sing, share a witness, and hear a message from someone adept at addressing teenagers. We even had a Bible club at the high school in those days. It was the largest of all the school clubs. I became a leader in this youth organization both in the school and at the rallies. Although I "preached" on occasion, my forte was song leading. I even won a national song-leading contest and spent the summer prior to my senior year with a youth team in Venezuela. Without a doubt, my faith and Christian service never seemed stronger or greater than during these high school years.

Part 2: College. I went to a Christian college because I wanted to prepare for a life in foreign missions. When I was six years old, I had been deeply touched by a young doctor preparing to be a medical missionary. This greatly influenced my desire to be a missionary. The summer in Venezuela only reinforced that desire, as did a meeting with the widow of one of four men who had recently been killed in Ecuador doing the kind of work I had felt called to do. I enrolled as a Greek major to prepare for Bible translation work among a people whose language had yet to be put into written form.

Three events mark my journey during college. First, because of my desire to have a genuine sense of God's presence in my life, I pursued a rigorous, disciplined life to grow spiritually, to know and experience God in a real way. My faith had been very cerebral, very rational; rarely at a visceral or gut level. I had been warned never to trust "experience" or "feelings," since they were unreliable witnesses to truth. The college years were a time to experiment with numerous spiritual disciplines in pursuit of spiritual growth. In fact, my greatest temptation then was not to do something wrong (and there were numerous, specified "wrongs" at my college!) but to do something right. I wanted to become spiritual for the power and acclaim that it would bring me with God and with my friends. But ironically the more I tried, the more control I took of my own life and the more manipulative I became in my relationship with God. Evil can raise its ugly head camouflaged in very attractive forms.

Second, after three years of "failure" to achieve the sought-after spiritual plateau, I enrolled in a philosophy of religion class. Already vulnerable, I let this course swing wide the floodgates of doubt. I felt that my head and my heart were misaligned, that the "faith" necessary to believe was too great a leap to make. I became a full-fledged rationalist. I devoured the writings of the humanist tradition. I looked at my Christian struggles as simply unenlightened attempts at discovering reality. "Man was the measure of all things." Dropping out of church and abandoning any semblance of Christianity, I became a humanist and felt a sense of relief.

At the end of that year and that class, the professor invited a humanist philosopher from another university to give a lecture in our class. I went eagerly to hear his critique of the Christian faith and his insight on the human condition. I listened to his critique with dismay and a growing uneasiness. Even more telling were his responses to the questions of my classmates. I realized then that it took more faith for this man to live with any sense of significance than for me to be a Christian. His view that we were at best "two lumps of clay sitting on a park bench sweating palm to palm" stunned me. I returned to the faith, but it was not the same as before. I had gained the freedom to question, to explore the formulas, the clichés, and the pat answers, to discover that God was so much different than the God of my early faith. I needed answers but not the same kind. I was willing to live with more ambiguity and with the possibility that there was more than one right answer—even the possibility that the "right" answers were not necessarily more important. I went to Scripture with an openness and a desire to face the questions that had often been dodged or repressed before. This was not an issue of doubt; it was now a part of my faith.

Third, in the spring of that same junior year, I made a trip to the Mayo Clinic to be examined for a congenital heart condition. I had lived with this defect since birth with little hope that I would ever reach adulthood. My folks had been candid with me and did not shelter or protect me. Ironically, though I assumed I had no future, I knew no physical constraints on the present. That gave me permission to live more and more with a "might be" and to prepare my college days to that end. At the Mayo Clinic, corrective surgery was suggested for the summer break.

Surgery was set. A brother of a staff person at my college was one of the nation's premiere cardiologists and pioneers in heart surgery. He agreed to take my case. I was in the best of hands. The night before surgery, however, I went to sleep not knowing whether I would fully awaken again alive or dead. Youth, health, and statistics were on my side. But as I lay there, I realized that my life was indeed in God's hands. Whether I lived or died, I *knew* that God was there. Rather than fear or anxiety, an inexplicable peace surrounded me. I had finally come to experience the reality of God in my gut. It was indeed the "peace that passes understanding."

Part Three: Postcollege. The dramatic experiences of my journey crammed into four years of college freed me to pursue many of the issues that had emerged. My life of faith has been a continual search for integrity—the merging of head and heart. After a master's degree in classics and a seminary degree that had begun to widen my horizons, I went into the German university environment to complete a doctorate in New Testament studies. I returned to the United States to teach and prepare seminarians for ministry, convinced of the validity of the gospel and of God's concern for the world expressed through the Church despite all its shortcomings. My work continually forced me, in encounters with students and the Church, to pursue the wedding of heart and head. I could never confess with my heart what my head could not affirm. But I know that it is not either/or but both/and.

After several years of seminary teaching and three years in parish ministry, I found myself faced with a different crisis of faith. My marriage of nearly sixteen years disintegrated. Many would assume that this crisis came from being in a setting and community where divorce would make you persona non grata. But for me the pain and crisis went much deeper. It involved the very heart of the gospel. I had believed, taught, and preached that God had acted in Christ to bring about restoration, healing, forgiveness, new life, and new beginnings for us all. But God was not working in my own marriage. Where was God when I really needed God? All that I had come to believe and "understand" was now on the line. For me there was only one way. But that way did not work out.

Angry with God, disillusioned with the gospel, I went to the president of the college and seminary to resign. He turned to me, a man with whom I had often differed regarding students and policies, and said, "Bob, I will not accept your resignation. We need you and you need us." This from the president of an institution that, until two years before, would not even admit a student or allow a student to continue should he or she be divorced. My other colleagues sensed the pain and anguish of soul and were there to encourage, support, and above all hold me up in prayer when I did not feel like praying at all. God became real to me, spoke to me, and made grace a part of my life through my colleagues. That is where I saw God's love and grace. For one who was always "right" and "righteous," one who wanted to be "spiritual" above all else, the scarlet letter of divorce has taught the meaning of grace. Never able to be "converted" because I knew so little of sin and failure, I have experienced God's accepting grace and found that my life is indeed in God's hands.

In recent years the terrain of my journey involved moving to the ministry of a local church from the academy that has always enthralled me and where I felt I had been uniquely equipped and gifted. I went against the "advice" of all my colleagues except one. Many of them still cannot understand why I made the move. I did not particularly want to do this. I certainly did not seek to do it and was relieved when the call committee initially turned to someone else. After all, I had an ideal teaching position in terms of my interests and sense of calling. When the church's call committee came back to ask me, however, all the obstacles, barriers, concerns that had stood in the way were removed. I felt there was no other choice. I did not "leave" an academic ministry, but "went" to become a teaching minister.

As this book goes to press, I have again accepted the call back into the academic setting. During the rich and intense years at Colonial Church, my one main anxiety was whether I would ever have the chance to return again to seminary teaching. White, male, middle-aged, and my interests being in New Testament studies seemed to stack the deck against me. But just as I had finally released my future to God and had entered a new year of ministry excited with the opportunities Colonial provided, the call came to return to teaching by joining the faculty at Fuller Theological Seminary in Pasadena, California.

I find myself at times still seeking to make a way, take control, make the future happen. The cutting edge remains "letting God be God" in my life and my future. My task, above all, is to be available and doing the ministry of helping others on their journeys of faith.

We encourage you at this point to stop and review your own journey of faith. Recall two or three of your most significant religious/spiritual experiences both before the age of twenty-one and after. Every story is different. We encourage all stories to be told. Your story belongs uniquely to you, and it provides the starting place from which to understand further the Critical Journey.

3

Stage 1:
The Recognition of God

"I feel closer to God in the garden than anywhere else on earth."

"My first experience of God was the day my brother miraculously recovered from stomach cancer. It was a real miracle."

"Standing on the mountain looking out at the other sharply defined, snow-covered peaks and the purple hues of the valley below and the azure blue sky above, I sense God's reality so much that I can't imagine anyone not believing in a Creator of it all."

Mom: *"I'm so glad your infection went away. Did you snuggle your Care Bear up close to your heart?"*
Four year old: *"No, I have Jesus close to my heart!"*

"About ten years ago I gave my life to Jesus. Working with a business associate on the West Coast, I was struck by her loving, joyful spirit —even under severe pressure and stress. One day I asked her if she was always so caring and joyful. She said she was. I then asked her what was her secret? She told me that Christ made the difference for her, and she told me how to ask him into my life. I was born again that day, and life has taken a very different tone for me ever since."

"Going through treatment for my chemical dependency was the first time I ever acknowledged that there is a power beyond me and that I am in need of daily assistance. AA is my experience of spirituality."

"When I saw the earth from out in space, I knew instantly that there was a God and that I needed to serve him."

"I never went to church at all when I was growing up. However, my grandmother did nurture me in the faith. She told me how God loved me and wanted good things for me. I think she represented God for me in my life."

"When I saw my infant son brought out of the delivery room, I knew beyond a shadow of doubt that there had to be Someone much bigger than my wife and me at work in this world."

Stage 1, the recognition of God, is where we all begin the journey of faith. We may experience it during early childhood or as adults who come for the first time to recognize the reality or presence of Someone who stands behind it all. Regardless of our age, however, it seems true that most begin the journey in a child-like way. We come to it with an innocence, a freshness, that is seldom ever again as vivid or vital.

Consider the way we feel during the first stage of a romance or new friendship. Swept away by the experience of the relationship, we do not look at any of the negative aspects. We are happy, perhaps a little silly and sleepless, restless to see the other person. It is a wonderful time, a time we may frequently long for again later in the relationship. Some are flush with the experience of discovery, as if they had found a surprise, a gift, a wonderful new person. For some, meeting God in this way becomes a peak event, a very identifiable, often datable, concrete life experience. For others, as in some romances that develop from a friendship, the recognition of this special relationship dawns so gradually that they aren't certain just where or when the experience began.

The experience of faith at this early stage is the discovery and *recognition of God*. It is accepting the fact of the reality of God in our lives. This is a very simple, though not always an easy, act. It requires no study or prerequisites. Frequently, it happens very naturally. We simply know that God is there. At times, it is a very conscious act, which is more characteristic of adults who enter the journey at this stage. There are a variety of ways to enter the journey and a variety of ways to be at this stage. To this we now turn our attention.

CHARACTERISTICS OF STAGE 1

We believe that people enter into a relationship with God in one of two very different ways. Some come through a sense of awe, others out of sense of need. We begin with these primary characteristics. The others tend to expand on these.

A SENSE OF AWE

Whatever route leads us to begin the spiritual journey, awe most likely underlies it at some point. Awe comes from being impressed with someone or something much larger than ourselves —in fact, bigger than life. Awe is that childlike quality in us that is amazed by someone or something. It is a delightful, endearing trait. It is a very comfortable state because it is so simple, so unquestioning, so real. It feels safe and secure like being wrapped in a parent's loving arms when exhausted by life or made anxious by its threats or pain.

For example, you can see this awe on the face of one who has just discovered for the first time, true and unconditional love. Tears and smile appear simultaneously. Consider this scene.

The scene takes place in a women's prison. The occasion is a weekend spiritual retreat focusing on unconditional love. Many hugs are exchanged. Deep connections of joy and pain are shared. Loving gifts are given. Prayers flow in from across the world. One woman's grief over the loss of her mother and another's grief over a daughter's illness are shared. Days are spent together. At the end of the long weekend one woman stands up and says through her tears, "God loves me. You people love me. No one has ever loved me before."

Children seem more likely to recognize God in their lives through awe than are adults. But whether as a child or an adult, when we recognize God to be God in our lives, we accept that Someone bigger than us truly loves us. We may experience God's love in many different ways even through other people. It could be someone who cares for us when we feel alone and rejected; someone who wants what is best for us despite our disappointments; someone who loves and forgives us when we mess up. Our response is one of awe, of yielding, accepting the reality and presence of God in our personal worlds.

A pleasant way to experience the awesomeness of God is to be present at a miracle: the birth of a child, the recovering of a person from cancer, the turnaround of a business in crisis, the successful treatment of chemical dependency, the saving of lives in a storm, the saving of a marriage about to dissolve. All of these events can inspire the awe of God as the power behind the event and may be determining factors in bringing us face to face with the awesomeness of God and starting us on our journey.

We can find numerous illustrations of this stage in the Scriptures. The Book of Proverbs is a collection of sayings that instruct about living in awe of God. Based on common sense, experience, and genuine wisdom, the proverbial sayings offer principles for living. But the collection begins with a proverb (Prov. 1:7) that sets all the other sage advice that follows in perspective: "The fear [awe] of the Lord is the beginning of knowledge." True wisdom takes God as God seriously.

The Hebrew Scriptures give many examples of the awe evoked from various people like Abraham, Moses, Sarah, Hannah, and Isaiah, who experience the presence of God. The prophet Isaiah's vision during his call is a classic. His vision of God evoked a tremendous sense of personal inadequacy. "Woe is me! For I am lost; for I am a man of unclean lips, and I dwell in the midst of a people of unclean lips; for my eyes have seen the King, the Lord of hosts" (Isa. 6:5). And several of the psalms speak with similar awe of God's greatness, goodness, power, and presence in words like "Great is the Lord and greatly to be praised in the city of our God, His holy mountain" (Ps. 48:1).

A SENSE OF NEED

When entering the journey as an adult, we frequently come out of a longing for a resolution to some discomfort. It may be a personal pain like divorce, an illness, a job loss, prison, grief, dependencies, abandonment, loneliness, or a search for meaning in life. We are really feeling scared, low and depressed, angry and bitter, or simply resigned. Alone in our pain, we feel unloved and unwanted. When God becomes real to us in this time of need, we find one who soothes us, loves and cares for us, and encourages us to go on living.

Recall a scene from the movie, *The Mission.* A former slave trader had killed his brother in a rage and had gone into deep depression from the pain and guilt of it all. He went to a priest but refused the offer of forgiveness. The priest then gave him a penance. He was to carry a heavy burden strapped to his back to a village accessible only by climbing a gigantic waterfall. After an arduous, treacherous, and exhausting climb with the priest, they finally arrived at the top of the waterfall. There they were greeted joyously by relatives of the villagers the slaver had previously kidnapped and sold into slavery. One young man recognized the once feared and hated slaver. He stepped forward and then graciously cut the burden loose from his back. The slaver broke down in a flood of tears. The simple relief and the acceptance of forgiveness by his enemies were overwhelming.

Perhaps, as the slave trader in *The Mission,* we meet God out of a sense of deep guilt that plagues us. We cannot go on very productively because the guilt is too debilitating. Meeting God, we let forgiveness sink into our guilt-ridden souls and accept the cleansing of God's acceptance as a true gift. Some of us would only consider spirituality if we were hurting in some way or had a personal need. When feeling successful or challenged in our lives, we are less likely to sense our need for God to lead us, heal us, or love us. We may be blinded to our inner needs when our outer lives are going so well.

A feeling of real rejection in life may bring us to God. That rejection may come through a loved one, our family, country, or race. We feel that life is simply not worth it, since we are ourselves worthless. Sometimes tragically we feel this rejection by a church or spiritual group. This is a most debilitating rejection because it leaves us in crisis with a spiritual need but no "spiritual base" to which to turn. Consequently, some turn to nonchurch or nonreligious bases to meet this need.

When we encounter God out of a deep need, it is as though we have been given life again because we truly accept that we are loved and accepted. So many disenfranchised people, abused people, poverty-stricken people, chronically ill people, chemically dependent people, divorced people, and abandoned people feel so desperately hopeless. Experiencing the overwhelming love of God saves their lives. In the Alcoholics Anonymous program, one of the first steps to sobriety is recognizing our powerlessness and need for a Higher Power.

Nothing expresses our dependence on God as adequately or more beautifully than "The Lord is my shepherd, I shall not want" from Psalm 23. The Gospels also contain many stories of people who turn in desperation to Jesus for help. Out of control and with no other recourse, they turn to Jesus to alleviate their suffering. For example, the leper in Mark 1:40–45 comes to Jesus to ask for "cleansing." His request reflects the social and religious onus of his disease that left him not only painfully crippled but ostracized by friends, family, and God. The woman plagued by a hemorrhage for twelve years had spent all her resources on physicians in a futile search for a cure. She risked the crowd and embarrassment to touch Jesus' clothes in a final hope for healing. Jesus in Mark 5:25–34 informs her that her "faith" had made her well.

A NATURAL AWARENESS

Some people at this stage clearly and completely experience God first through their senses. We are not given to *thinking* about God. Rather we simply experience the presence of God. We can see God in the sunrise over a cool summer lake. We can hear God in the cry and coo of a newborn baby. The scent of the first spring flowers bears God to us. Some feel God in the soft velvet of the altar cloth warmed by the burning candle and sense God's presence in worship or the liturgy. And some experience God in the creative process. In other words, we do not experience God's presence primarily in a rational way but in an experiential way, using the various senses.

Frequently, nature will provide our initial entrée to the spiritual journey. Sometimes we may even wonder if we are really on the journey, since we have no recollection of a specific time, place, or situation in which we first encountered God. We experience God in a natural, rather than a supernatural, way. We may not have had any crisis or awesome experience, although we feel a genuine sense of awe through nature. The rushing brook invigorates us; the ocean surf and breeze relax us; a hike in the woods clears our minds; the lighting of a log fire inspires us; the warmth of the sun soothes us. We are not sure what causes these feelings, but we attribute them to nature and thus we long for nature frequently. Or we see God in nature and long to experience God more in these ways.

We who know God through a sense of God's presence in nature find that simply being in nature brings out our simple childlike selves. We become more ourselves, more satisfied and less anxious and repressed. We experience a yearning to be in the woods or on a lake, to be climbing, bird watching, or whatever, knowing that we have a sense of fulfillment and oneness with the Creator. There is nowhere else that we feel just that way. Our inner nature is revealed in our experiences of nature externally.

One experience we may easily overlook as spiritual is our creativity. The inspiration behind a drawing, a poem, a play, a dance, a painting, a story, a weaving, a gourmet meal, a product of our design and/or manufacture, or a speech can come from God. The whole creative process can be guided by God, and it can change the style and intent of the product and process. Even creativity can be enriched by simply letting go.

Again the psalmist illustrates this awareness and speaks of the whole creation reacting in praise to God: the stars, the heavens, the seas and their inhabitants, fire, hail, snow and frost, mountains, hills, trees, birds, and animals (Psalm 48). And Jesus points to the "lilies of the field" and the "birds of the air" to illustrate God's presence in and provision for all of creation (Matt. 6:26–30). Paul in his letter to the Roman Christians reminds them that God's person and power are revealed through nature even to those who have never heard about God. "Ever since the creation of the world his invisible nature, namely, his eternal power and deity, has been clearly perceived in the things that have been made" (Rom. 1:20).

GREATER MEANING IN LIFE

Some people experience this stage as the fulfillment of a longing or desire to get deeper into life, to penetrate beyond the surface, the superficial. We seek more significance from life than we presently are experiencing. Many have had no previous "faith" experiences and simply want to live life more intensely. We sense there is something more but have no idea what it is or how to find it. Someone, usually a friend, introduces us to a "spiritual" experience of some kind, perhaps even without naming it as a religious or faith event. Yet we know that we have experienced Someone or Something, though we may not be able to name the Whirlwind. For example, a crisis resolved at work or a psychological breakthrough in therapy may elicit that response. We may not be able to name this as an experience of faith, a recognition of God as God, until we are at a later phase of the journey and look back and see God's hand in our lives.

The story of Zacchaeus (Luke 19:1–10) offers a biblical illustration of one for whom life had paid rich dividends. He had found great success in the nether world of taxes. But he was intrigued by reports about Jesus and his ministry. His curiosity piqued, he climbed a tree to get a better vantage point to take a look at Jesus when he came to town. To his consternation, Jesus singled him out and invited himself to Zacchaeus's house for dinner. Suddenly, conscious that his way of life was terribly wrongheaded, Zacchaeus pledged to find a new orientation for his life and even repay with interest any he might have defrauded. Jesus declared, "Today salvation [wholeness] has come to this house" (Luke 19:9).

A SENSE OF INNOCENCE

Stage 1 elicits a ready acceptance of anything having to do with God. Because we feel so awed, and we accept the fact that our faith is itself a miracle, we want to live in this unconditional acceptance wherever we are. We often believe that the world is all in God's hands and that all people will love others, if given a chance. The childlike faith says, "God accepts and forgives me, can't you?" We believe our lives are orchestrated by God, whose perfect will promises harmony and peace for all who follow God. Enthused by our relationship with God, we try to bring out the best in others through our encouragement and our kind hearts. We trust people implicitly, especially those who share our faith. We seldom question them, nor do we notice any evil in others. We are truthful. We are loving.

The fresh confidence of this phase echoes through the words of the young David in the familiar Bible story when he watched with horror as the giant Goliath successfully challenged and frightened the army of Israel. David could not believe that no one would step forward. He asked incredulously, "Who is this uncircumcised Philistine, that he should defy the armies of the living God?" When King Saul asked David about his presumptuous words, he answered, "Let no man's heart fail because of [Goliath]; your servant will go and fight with this Philistine" (1 Sam. 17:32). And when he met Goliath his complete faith in God's help comes through his words: "You come to me with a sword and with a spear and with a javelin; but I come to you in the name of the Lord of hosts, the God of the armies of Israel, whom you have defied. This day the Lord will deliver you into my hand" (1 Sam. 17:45–46).

In a touching scene from Jesus' ministry, Luke 18:14–17 tells us how Jesus rebuked his friends one day because they sought to prevent parents from bringing "even infants to him that he might touch them" (Luke 18:15). He invited the children to come to him, "for to such belongs the kingdom of God" and told his followers that "whoever does not receive the kingdom of God like a child shall not enter it" (Luke 18:16–17).

EXAMPLES OF OUR JOURNEY IN STAGE ONE

Janet: I first experienced God through my early Sunday school classes and learned more about God from a sense of need than a sense of awe (unless awe means abject fear). God was pictured as the Big Old White-Haired Man on the throne, wanting my obedience. I was the sinner, in need of forgiveness. Of course, love was mentioned, and I experienced God's love in many ways, through many people, especially my mother. But at ages three to five the Authoritative Father impressions and images stayed with me. I was raised with respect of God but little sense of intimacy. This need-oriented approach characterized my relationship to God throughout my early childhood. It was my home stage until my elementary school years.

I returned to this stage as home base twice in times of great need. The first time was when my mother died. I was twenty-two and had become agnostic. In this crisis, I knew I could not return to my childhood faith. Consequently, I spent a lot of time searching for God in psychology. I had a great need for faith but not what I called "religion." So God appeared to me in psychology. My counseling training, which nurtured me toward being a mentally healthy person, was God at work in my life in a time of great need. The second time of great need was after my divorce. I once again experienced a deep sense of loss of meaning in life. I felt a great need and turned to God again, this time through reading, meditation, and simple prayer. I was so lonely and felt at times that only God wanted to be with me. My friends were God's loving presence in my life, and I also found, by chance, a faith community that accepted me, included me, and loved me. I felt like I had a home and that I didn't have to be any certain way to be accepted. It was the first time I had been in a faith community that fit me in years.

Though this stage is no longer my home stage, I now experience it regularly. I feel a sense of awe and love for God as I see God's hand in many parts of my life. I experience God in reflective, quiet times, when sitting on my deck listening to the birds or at work writing. But I am more awed to sense God in the middle of busy days, in the middle of conversations or consultations.

I am awed by the patience I am receiving, since patience is not one of my virtues. I am awed by the tolerance of my family and friends for my unusual qualities. I am struck by the humor of life I find all around me. I laugh a lot more than I used to. In general when I experience this stage now, I feel more childlike than ever before.

Allen: I was a homebuilder, building a lot of homes, and I had accumulated on paper a certain amount of wealth. When interest rates went to 22 percent I lost everything. Because of that and other problems in the past, my wife and I divorced. I was really hurting. As far as homebuilding was concerned, I was able to put together a kitchen cabinet and bath cabinet display room, selling to homebuilders, individuals, and remodelers. My new business was moving right along and doing well when all of a sudden my two largest accounts went bankrupt.

There I was on the bottom again, but this time it was worse. They had given me some checks for quite a few thousand dollars just before they filed for bankruptcy, and I deposited these checks, using the money to pay employees, suppliers, and my own account. I was charged by the Attorney General's office with fraud because I should have known their checks were not good. It wasn't long before I knew I would be serving time in prison. I felt desperate.

I had known Jim Farmer for a number of years. I'd done some business with him. We were good friends, and one day, in fact it was January 19, I was in his office thanking him for what he'd done for me. I had this note along with me saying that I was going to end it all, and when I left Jim's office, I left this note on his desk. He could tell that I was troubled that day and something was wrong. I guess I was screaming out for help, but I didn't realize it at the time. He grabbed the note, and as I headed out the door, he grabbed me and got me back in his office. We had a long discussion about why I shouldn't do this, and he said, "Allen, you need some help. You need somebody to talk to. Let me call my church."

He got hold of Helen, and they arranged for me to come down to meet with her at 1:30. After we had talked for awhile, she said, "I want to get Ralph." So she went out to catch him. It is kind of strange how God works. Ralph was supposed to have had an appointment around 2:30 downtown, and he'd gotten a call at 1:30, about the same time I was walking through the door, canceling his appointment. He came in and joined us, and we talked until around 6:00. Ralph pointed out to me the fact that God did not make junk, and that committing suicide was an easy out for me. Regardless of how my family felt at the time, they would end up suffering for years. Was this really fair? Ralph and Helen showed me that I did have some God-given talents that would be wasted if I did go through with it, and that they were willing to help me and be close even while I was in prison. And they would be there waiting for me when I came out.

So I decided that was the thing to do, go through with prison. While I was there I got counseling. And I got to know the chaplain out there. We hit it off. We got well acquainted. He knew that there was a need for some things to go on in the chapel and got me involved, and we just had a chance to visit a lot.

Also while I was in prison, I got involved with the people from Helen and Ralph's church who came out there once a month. Right after I got there, Ralph was out just to see me and to bring me a Bible. Support from all these people kept me going.

Well, I got out on Labor Day. I was driven out to "my church" on Sunday morning, and I didn't realize that services were at a different time. I was standing in the hallway, and the services ended. Ralph and Helen were walking out of church, when Ralph spotted me, he let out a yell to Helen, "Look who's here!" And that was the start of a real change in my life.

CAGED AT STAGE ONE

WORTHLESSNESS

We can get stuck at this stage or caged when, instead of feeling love and awe, we think of God and others as constantly having expectations of us that we cannot measure up to. We dwell on having failed others or are certain we shall fail them. We feel worthless. Nothing that others say to be supportive seems honest. If they only knew us well enough, they would not say such nice things about us. Constantly feeling guilt or shame for our behavior, we see no way to change. Consequently, we tend to mistrust others, especially those close to us. We can even become paranoid.

We may have developed this attitude about ourselves from childhood, from home or school or church. We see no way we can get better or measure up again. One woman said, "I can't go to church because I feel people can see right into me and see how dirty I am."

SPIRITUAL BANKRUPTCY

Feeling personally or spiritually bankrupt is another expression of being caged at stage 1. There is nothing there; no well to draw from; no energy left. We feel that no one cares for us— certainly not God, because if God really cared, we would be rescued. We look for miracles but know they will never occur for us. We do not deserve them. We feel we have nowhere to turn and even God is not listening. We are not sufficient to ask for anything.

MARTYRDOM

Suffering or martyrdom often typifies the way of life for those caged here. We feel the whole world is out to make life tough for us, to hurt us, humiliate us, to get us and certainly not to help, love or care for us. Unconsciously, we think we deserve what comes but it angers us nonetheless. Frequently, when caged at this stage we carry a lot of anger but cannot deal with it. We cover it by heaping more harsh treatment on ourselves. We may even think our faith in God should bring about suffering, persecution, and misunderstanding for we are then being persecuted for God's sake. Somehow joy, happiness, peace are not to be our lot because we do not feel we deserve such.

IGNORANCE

Ignorance about faith issues also marks those caged at this stage. Why try to understand or learn about such matters, since it would be of little use? Feeling incapable of experiencing great thoughts, we shy away from the struggle. It corresponds with our low self-esteem.

At stage 1, God is often taken as the great, heavenly Magician. This can lead to caged behavior. For example, we might be doing nothing to help ourselves in a problem situation and then complain that God was not there for us. As someone once said, "God can't steer a parked car." Superstitions fit here too. Fear that God will make you ill, if you fail to pray regularly. Or belief that you will have success, if you "play the game by God's rules."

A light story illustrates this point. A man during personal crisis opened the Bible at random to find God's "word" of advice for him. His eye fell immediately on "And Judas went out and hanged himself." Thinking this was just a fluke and certainly not meant for him, he tried again. Opening the Bible at random and pointing to another verse, he read, "Go thou and do likewise." Troubled, he decided to give it one last try. To his amazement, he pointed to "What thou doest, do quickly!" His magical faith had left him in a quandary.

People stuck at stage 1 can give an impression of being very pious. In reality, we suffer greatly because we feel so disconnected from God. So afraid, we cannot talk easily about our alienation. Fear of rejection (from low self-esteem) represents the predominant feeling in this cage. As a result of fear and self-abasement, we frequently become aggressive toward ourselves (unforgiving and self-centered in controlling ways) or passively aggressive toward others by hurting them through what we do not do, will not say, or say behind their backs. Acting naively, we really want control and feel afraid of losing it. We become almost desperate to hang on to the shreds of continuity we have, even if they are damaging to us.

Ironically, in this stage, the very behavior that initially brought people to a recognition of God can become a cage for them. For instance, a grave sense of need. If in recognizing God and beginning the journey we do not accept that God can help answer our needs out of love and care; if we reject God's overtures to us, we can become caged in rigorous self-defeating behavior. If, in our utter awe of God, we do not move toward this source of joy, we can let ourselves become overwhelmed, inadequate and gradually less worthwhile. Our strength in approaching God has turned against us. One help at this point is to reach out to others who can support us, understand us, and help us stay on the journey.

MOVING FROM STAGE ONE TO STAGE TWO

Become Part of a Strong Group Support seems to be the key to how people move from the first to the second stage. We become part of a strong group of like people or believers with whom we are comfortable. We ease into a sense of belonging. We feel cared about and we begin to feel more significant. This can happen within a variety of settings from classes, AA groups, Bible studies, retreat groups, support groups, sports groups, community groups, nature groups, social friendship groups, or a church.

Let Life Take on More Significance If you entered the journey from a point of deep need and you wondered about life's significance, the movement to stage 2 can signify to you that life indeed is meaningful, if only because other people seem to like you, and God loves you. Perhaps just acknowledging that there is indeed something worth working for is a major move toward the belonging stage.

Find a Charismatic Leader to Follow Many find the move to the second stage strongly tied with the recognition of and a desire to follow a significant leader, or belief system. Usually the belief system is led by or was started by a writer, preacher, teacher, or gifted person. At this point we want and need to be led, taught, discipled. We naturally find the gifted person or principle to provide that for us. We discover and gratefully subscribe to *the* way through the leader, writings, creeds, Scripture, or a special group. It is comfortable and exhilarating to belong, to be part of something bigger than we are.

Discover the Way For a long time we may have been isolated in searching for the way God has in store for us to grow. Now, we stumble upon a set of ideas, a belief system or a group of people who show us the light and answer our questions. It is such a big relief and feels so safe and secure—like a haven in a storm. And for now, that is what we need.

THE CRISIS OF MOVEMENT FROM
STAGE ONE TO TWO

The movement from one stage to the next is frequently uncomfortable or at least confusing as we explained in chapter 1. During each movement we have to overcome or acknowledge certain things, thus helping us to move. Because movement between stages is felt either as a crisis or a big change by most people, we will describe the major requirements of moving as crises of movement between stages, or what can keep us from moving to the next stage.

Accept Self-Worth The movement from stage 1 to stage 2 requires an acknowledgement that we are basically worthwhile human beings and that we are loved just as we are. This means we may have to give up some spiritually self-defeating behavior and accept God's love and care.

Reduce Isolation Second, we need to accept the caring of the community that is reaching out to us if we are to find belonging. We need to move out of isolation. We need to move toward community without knowing exactly why, only that it feels like a necessary thing.

SUMMARY OF STAGE 1:
THE RECOGNITION OF GOD

Thesis: Faith is the discovery or recognition of God.

Characteristics of Stage 1

A Sense of Awe

A Sense of Need

A Natural Awareness

Greater Meaning in Life

A Sense of Innocence

Caged at Stage 1

Worthlessness, Spiritual Bankruptcy,
Martyrdom, Ignorance

Moving from Stage 1 to Stage 2

Become Part of a Strong Group, Let Life
Take on More Significance, Find a Charismatic
Leader to Follow, Discover *the* Way

Crisis of Movement

Accept Self-Worth; Reduce Isolation

Question

How and when did you first recognize God
in your life? (Awe or need?)

EXPERIENCING STAGE 1

QUESTIONS

1. How do you experience God most, by awe, a sense of need, nature, or a search for greater meaning? Explain.
2. When have you recognized or felt God strongly in your life?
3. What (if any) is your tangible symbol of God's presence in your life (e.g., a candle, a picture, a poem, a person)?

EXERCISES

1. Read the story of the leper (Mark 1:40–45) or the story of the woman with a hemorrhage (Mark 5:25–34). Imagine yourself in the scene as the man or woman approaching Jesus. Listen to yourself and listen to Jesus as you seek healing and help. Write your reactions and observations into a personal journal, or speak them into a tape recorder.
2. Read this psalm over very slowly in your mind or into a tape recorder. Let each word sink in and observe your awareness.

The Lord is my shepherd, I shall not want;
   he makes me lie down in green pastures.
He leads me beside still waters;
   he restores my soul.
He leads me in the paths of righteousness
   for his name's sake.
Even though I walk through the valley of the shadow
      of death,
   I fear no evil;
for thou art with me;
   thy rod and thy staff, they comfort me.

Thou preparest a table before me
   in the presence of my enemies;
thou anointest my head with oil,
   my cup overflows.
Surely goodness and mercy shall follow me
   all the days of my life;
and I shall dwell in the house of the Lord
   for ever.

3. Take a walk in the woods, by a lake or the beach, in the mountains, anywhere you like, and wait for God to surprise you with something from the vast storehouse of nature: perhaps a small wild flower, a surge of waves, a bird singing, a bright color, peaceful winds, utter calm. Let the awe of God, God's presence, touch you. Try capturing these feelings or experiences by forming a picture of them in your mind or by writing them in a journal.

4. Explore for a moment where you find meaning in your own life. Put it in writing: things, people, experiences, activities. What is most important for you? Then divide them into categories such as work, relationships, leisure pursuits. In terms of time spent, which category stands out? What about the quantity of items? Is God or your experience of faith mentioned? Reflect a moment on your list. What we derive meaning from actually determines our way of living.

4

Stage 2:
The Life of Discipleship

"When I am in nature, I feel I am being taught, instructed in its ways, and it is for me to be observant and to obey. It is all there, repeating itself over and over, and it all pertains to my life."

"I love my faith because it is so clear what I am to believe and how I am to act. The Bible answers my questions, and my church has clear teachings that have become the rules for my life."

"My friends in the Cursillo group are the most important people in my life. They make faith come alive. They are there for me when I need them. They're loving and real. I belong. They miss me when I'm gone. I am part of something bigger than myself."

"Our pastor gives us clear teaching on the life of faith and issues we should be involved with. He knows God's Word so well, and we are ready to learn from him. That's why we're here. We need sound instruction and community issues to work on. And we're so fortunate to have him as our pastor.

"I would not call myself religious because the Church isn't it for me. But I'm definitely on a spiritual journey. I get together with others who are too. We explore all kinds of spirituality—other forms, other brands so to speak, and other processes. We are all seeking to learn and come to truths for ourselves."

"I am new in the faith. I need to know where to go to find the right answer for my many questions. There are so many different view-points that I am somewhat confused. How can I know what's really right?"

"The Church has often made God too confined. I want a broader concept of God, one freed from the provincialism of the Church."

This stage is best characterized as a time of learning and belonging. No matter which faith group we have entered at stage 1, whether nature oriented or high church, stage 2 frees us to explore, to learn, to quest, to absorb, to put into place our set of beliefs or faith principles. In this stage we learn the most about God as perceived by others we respect and trust. We are apprentices. It is a time to be with other people in that process, a social time with companion searchers on the journey. Because we are relatively unsure and insecure at first in our growth and in what we believe, it is very useful to include others in this phase. In fact it is crucial to this phase of the journey. We are taught by others. Sometimes we learn from getting together and talking, or sometimes we learn from others' writings.

At this stage, we clearly are the learners, not the teachers. This is a taking stage, a filling stage. It feels very much like a one-way street. This means vulnerability, and some feelings of fear and even inadequacy accompany the excitement of new learning. But the group, the sense of others learning too, helps mitigate those feelings. We learn to be obedient disciples; to trust the teacher or leader and to be as much like them as possible.

CHARACTERISTICS OF STAGE 2

MEANING FROM BELONGING

Being open to friendship and companionship from others on the journey makes a big difference at this stage. Those from and with whom we journey clearly determine what and how we experience this phase of our faith. It usually is a relief to find others on the journey where we are. It feels so good to be with people who understand us. Our acceptance in our faith community is largely determined by how open we are and how well we resonate to the overtures of the group.

We will see this belonging phenomenon traditionally portrayed where one finds distinctly different belief systems underlying various churches and synods within churches. Sometimes the language we use or the way in which we say the Lord's Prayer determines which group we have allegiance to. We know who "we" are and who "they" are. We feel most safe, content, and comfortable with "we" and less comfortable with "them." The group gives us our sense of identity and security.

As small children, many people experience this stage in Sunday school where week after week we absorbed stories, ideas, Bible verses, the distinctive beliefs of the Church, without even knowing at times what it all meant. Concepts like justification, venial sins, sanctification, omniscience, and even salvation are often too abstract to be relevant to the adolescent child. Yet it is important to learn and absorb tradition. Memory verses, for example, learned at age eight or ten will often stay with us to be recalled much later. Being schooled in the teaching of the church, including special words, is often part of belonging and being accepted, of passing the test.

We can have a sense of belonging and association on the journey of faith without being a member of a traditionally defined religious community. It may even be an association of similar people in overt reaction against the traditional community of faith. For some it is the pursuit of social causes and issues that unites them in a community. We may not think the cause is "spiritual," but we pursue it with religious zeal. In some cases, the belonging consists in finding some who share our feelings and thoughts and aid us in exploring them further, like an AA group. This may be stimulated by a search for something that is genuine or simply a time of learning to articulate our intellectual skepticism. The point remains that the group gives us support and helps shape our identity.

The critical role that belonging plays at this stage can be

sensed when, after a period of time away from our community of faith, we return with the feeling that we are now home again. This is family. We are loved and accepted. Despite the struggles that go with community, there is good feeling that these are "my kind of people."

Frequently, there are groups within groups that give a strong sense of belonging at this stage. Most faith communities deliberately try to break themselves into smaller units to allow people to know one another better and to share their lives and faith more readily. There are many examples. Small groups are created for social contact (the women's circles and men's breakfast groups); for education (Bible studies and seminars of all sorts that offer answers to questions about living the life of faith); for work (task forces, boards, and committees); for special interests (choirs, physical fitness, and church sport teams); for counseling (aimed toward personal and interpersonal growth); and for support (grief, separation/divorce, unemployment, career changes, major illnesses or addiction, and retirement as well as spiritual renewal). The more traditional forms of Sunday school classes, youth groups, church camps, and retreat experiences stand out for many as formative associations in their journeys of faith. Through all of these settings, we experience God through association with others. The group forms our concepts of who and what God is. Often key figures, particular leaders, exhibit what we are seeking to experience. They become models for us.

A classic example of faith by association lies in the role Israel played as the People of God in the Hebrew Scriptures. They had a clear definition of their neighbor as one who shared the same heritage, rituals, and customs. And within Judaism in Jesus' day, there were groups who viewed themselves as the true Israel based on their own teachings about the Law and their interpretation of the Scriptures. Most prominent were the Pharisees, who represent Jesus' arch opponents, and the Essenes, who separated themselves in the desert community of Qumran away from the rest of Judaism.

ANSWERS FOUND IN A LEADER, CAUSE, OR
BELIEF SYSTEM

At stage 2 one thing is clear. We are not confident in ourselves to know what to believe or how to learn about God and know God better. We are dependent on a more advanced person in the faith or a guiding principle or cause to lead us and tell us the way to a fuller life.

Some look to Mother Nature for instruction. We wait in awe to be led to new insights, to be taught by the birds, to be tricked by the squirrels, to be put in danger by storms, to be quieted by a rushing stream. We sense in a deep, spiritual way that we are not in control of nature. We feel our best when in tune with nature and the universe. Our tendency is to try in myriad ways to control nature, both within us and around us. But all to no avail. We are the students; nature is the teacher.

We look to leaders of causes to shape us. We sense some charisma, some special enlightenment, an emotional, spiritual or intellectual depth that we attribute to the leader or cause that we follow. The person may be a pastor, priest, writer, lay leader, parent, singer, prophet, or muse. We are entranced by their qualities, usually feeling deep inside that we would like to be more like them. Therefore, we listen and follow what they say. We are learning the way of discipleship; learning to follow and heed the advice and instruction of others.

For some, a cause itself is so compelling, it becomes the leader, telling us what principles and behavior to follow. Hunger relief, evangelism, wellness, peace, healing, and missions represent causes to which we ascribe. We eagerly seek to become adept in language and behavior to serve the cause.

At this stage people see the cause or leader as *the* answer because it has truly enlightened or changed them. They become enthusiastic to see others have the same experience so they too can find satisfaction. Confusion or disappointment may arise when others don't seem to have the same experience after hearing their leader speak, reading their books, or accompanying them to meetings, workshops, or seminars.

The familiar story of Nicodemus who came to Jesus by night illustrates how one can be attracted by a powerful figure. He recognized Jesus to be a "Rabbi, . . . a teacher come from God" (John 3:2). On another occasion, a scribe came to Jesus and boldly said, "I will follow you wherever you go" (Matt. 8:19). He recognized Jesus as an authority figure, a teacher from whom he wanted to learn. And Paul referred to different groups within the church of Corinth who had rallied around the person and instruction of Cephas (Peter), Apollos, Paul, and Christ (1 Cor. 1:12).

SENSE OF RIGHTNESS

At stage 2 the phrase "I found it" best describes the feelings we have. First, *I* found it. No one found it for me, nor could they find it for me. I feel delighted and fortunate to have discovered *the way* and want to learn more about it and how to live it. Second, I *found* it. What was unknown to me, hidden from me has been discovered. I was lost but now I'm found. I'm accepted, reinstated, real. I experience my faith as a gift, a treasure to be relished after a long quest for *the* answer for my life. Third, I found *it*. I know this is right, the right way. I have total confidence in the strong leader to be my guide or in the justness of the cause or the answer. This is a good feeling that gives zest to life. Certainty brings a sense of relief and honor. We often take pride in our certainty, a certainty that is shared by others with whom we are at home. Having found the way, we are beset less by doubts and fears. My conviction sustains me even during troubling times because I have the answers to turn to, people to support and reinforce me in doing what needs to be done. It is very comforting, and gives me confidence.

At the beginning of the Gospel of John, we read about the gathering of the disciples around Jesus. In a vignette of two lesser-known disciples, Philip, who had just been personally called by Jesus to join the group, finds a man named Nathanael and enthusiastically recruits him by declaring "We have found him of whom Moses in the law and also the prophets wrote,

Jesus of Nazareth, the son of Joseph" (John 1:45). So convinced was Philip that he challenged Nathaniel to "Come and see" when the latter dared raise a question about Philip's find. In a similar way, the notorious Samaritan Woman at the Well came to discover the answer for her life through her conversation with Jesus. She then went to her village and invited the people to "Come, see a man who told me all that I ever did" (John 4:29). She too had found the answer, and it had changed her life.

SECURITY IN OUR FAITH

There is comfort at this stage, knowing that we personally do not have to figure out the answers since someone else can help us with them. Finding out what the workable answers are for us is a relief. There is a feeling of being safe, not having to worry because there is somewhere to go, someone who knows, a set of guidelines, a group that supports us. It feels like having huge hands under us, everlasting arms supporting us all along the journey, even when crises occur.

Many people clearly describe their life of faith at this stage as "comfortable." We do not feel yet like launching into any uncertainty. We want to rely on others and draw on them. It feels safe and just plain comfortable to be here. We know we are loved, and we trust our community of Christian friends.

A wonderful example of this is the comforting section of each Gideon Bible that lists where to turn in the text when in need. It covers everything, including grief, suicide, joy, the bad times, and new birth. It shows graphically that there are answers for each need. We are never alone, never without comfort, if we but choose to seek it. It is only our own negligence or doubt that keeps us from knowing help or comfort at this stage.

Whereas at stage 1 we feel awe and a deep sense of love, at stage 2 we know more about why that is the case. We are more confident of the faith as it is taught to us, and we are clearly on the road to more understanding and greater spiritual growth. Being with others who believe as we do, who help us, accept us, push us, love us, and even cajole us enhances our spiritual journey. We know we can make it if we are faithful.

In the beautiful story of Naomi and Ruth, Ruth, the daughter-in-law, refused to return to her family and her previous religious setting with the familiar words: "Entreat me not to leave you or to return from following you; for where you go I will go, and where you lodge I will lodge; your people shall be my people, and your God my God" (Ruth 1:16). The Apostle Paul graphically and repeatedly makes the point with reference to our own security. "Who shall separate us from the love of Christ? Shall tribulation, or distress, or persecution, or famine, or nakedness, or peril, or sword? No. . . . For I am sure that neither death, nor life, nor angels, nor principalities, nor things present, nor things to come, nor powers, nor height, nor depth, nor anything else in all creation, will be able to separate us from the love of God in Christ Jesus our Lord" (Rom. 8:35–39). "I know whom I have believed, and I am sure that he is able to guard until that Day what has been entrusted to me" (2 Tim. 1:12).

EXAMPLES OF JOURNEYS AT STAGE 2

Bob: I have experienced this stage in my own journey at various times. As a young person, I belonged to a church that had a strong sense of its identity. This identity came through what we believed and how we lived. Our belief system was clearly formulated. Belonging meant believing and expressing what we believed in a certain way with certain words and phrases. Consequently, learning what we believed and being able to give expression to what we believed had a lot to do with our standing in the community of faith. Our lifestyle was equally important in determining our place in the community. The lifestyle meant doing many church-related things, like attending church regularly. "Regularly" meant every time there was a scheduled service (at least twice on Sunday and Wednesday evenings). It meant giving our tithe of 10 percent and a "love offering" of even more. Naturally, it meant reading and studying the Bible, prayer, sharing our faith, and fellowship with the group. It also meant not doing things that were considered worldly or unbecoming a Christian. These standards were set by the community of faith, and our standing in the group depended on how well we lived up to these standards.

Since I have always been keen to learn and am a chronic "pleaser," this stage was a natural for me, especially during my early teenage years. I sought to learn as much as I could about what I should believe and how to best express it. At the same time, I sought willingly to order my life according to the principles set by the community so that I might be acceptable both to the group and ultimately to God. I wanted to think and do what was "right."

In more recent years, I have learned how important it is to have a community of faith with whom to identify and to share my journey. The emphasis for me now is more in the sense of community of shared life and faith than on the "learning." I have even found that the needs of this stage can best be met not by belonging to the right church as such, but by a group of people within a church or from several churches with whom I can share my journey and whose journeys I can share for my enrichment. Learning still takes place. But it comes more in the form of discovery and enrichment as we share our journeys of faith.

Lorraine: I left the church for seventeen years and had no relationship with God except to say "Help me" when I was in trouble.

During those years I had married, and as that relationship ended, the one huge benefit I felt was that I was being drawn to seek out a life with God again. I was excited about the prospect and started church hunting. The church I now attend was the second church I visited, and from the first Sunday I knew I'd found a home. It was only later that I realized over the past six years on four different occasions someone had tried to influence me to attend there—the only church that had ever been suggested. Not only did I feel that healing could take place there, I strongly believed that God wanted me at that particular church. I encountered my ex-husband there the second Sunday I attended, which brought some painful memories, and yet I never doubted this was the environment God had chosen for my healing and growth.

The worship services opened up the door—whetted my appetite and I discovered I had been starving. When the fall activities booklet came I was like a kid in a candy store trying to figure out what to attend first. I had been away *so* long. When I came back to God after all those years I was overwhelmed that he cared enough to wait for me—to come and get me—to give me a chance to pick up where I left off.

The first course I took was on prayer as it relates to your personality type. God had control of that choice—I had intended to attend another lecture, which was held on the same night, and changed my mind at the last minute. The prayer class clarified many things for me. It told me that some experiences I had had as a young person that seemed to defy logic really *were* spiritual experiences. It freed me to accept those experiences as real and valid. That understanding set the foundation for my journey.

After accepting my spiritual self and finding support in some of the church programs for that part of me, I realized I needed to know more about everything. I bought a study Bible and started reading Scripture voluntarily (a totally new experience). I enrolled in a Bible study group. I attended Sunday morning Bible study.

There are so many more steps I've taken on this journey, but these are probably the most significant. Part of the song "He's Everything to Me" sums up this journey of mine:

> Till by faith I met him face to face,
> And I felt the wonder of his grace
> Then I knew that he was more than just a God who
>   didn't care,
>   who lived away up there,
> And now he walks beside me day by day,
> Ever watching o'er me lest I stray,
> Helping me to find the narrow way,
> He's everything to me.

CAGED AT STAGE 2

RIGID IN RIGHTEOUSNESS

It is very seductive at this stage to believe that what is right for us in the faith is what is right for everyone else as well. We often believe that the religious or moral rules by which we live as a faithful disciple should be followed by everyone else. There is a tendency to become legalistic and moralistic, rigid in our understanding of what is right and what is wrong. Punishment of offenders can become an obsession with those caged at stage 2. Whatever the group's orientation, whether liberal, conservative, or in between, its teachings, doctrines, codes of conduct must be adhered to or the offender is alienated.

This behavior in the liberal wing of the Church is particularly paradoxical. Espousing acceptance of a wide range of views and behavior, they exclude from their circle of acceptance people who are narrower. The more conservative side often substantiates their viewpoint from Scripture to make it unarguable. No one caged in this lack of acceptance sees their own rigidity. It is impossible for them to see it, since they are so sure they are right. Consequently, a group arrogance develops, which is actually counterproductive to their cause but which they seldom notice.

WE AGAINST THEM

The strong sense of belonging and community characteristic of stage 2 can change to caged behavior in which one becomes stuck in a very closed, esoteric, paranoid, overly protective group. There develops a strong sense of "we" versus "them." Anyone in the group is good; those outside our group are bad. Suspicion can fester and grow until it gets out of proportion. The final stage of paranoia produces cults. This becomes inevitably destructive. Becoming more and more isolated in their own environment, people in cults lose touch with reality. The power of the leader takes on unrealistic proportions that can become unhealthy and even deadly.

THE SWITCHERS

We join a group that looks very much alive and ready to meet our needs or beliefs as we have come to recognize them. We join, participate, and live in the group for a time. But then gradually we come to realize that the group is not exactly what we had been looking for. We grow disillusioned with it and criticize it. We accuse the group of changing and fault it for not being for us what we really need. It may be that the leader has begun to move in a different direction than the one we found or thought we found upon joining. So we leave. We may try initially to make changes or voice our difference, but to no avail. We feel betrayed. While we have kept the beliefs or lived the faith in our perception, others in the group or the leader have not. Our security is threatened. We then switch to another group that now appears to be more in keeping with our needs, beliefs, or ideals.

On the spiritual journey we Switchers spend a great deal of time at this stage because we continually change from one group to another. We are not moving *on* in our journey, but we are moving around, and the movement gives us a sense of progress along the way. Often we experience intense highs and lows because joining and leaving are such emotional events. That very intensity may be one of the reasons we switch. At the same time, the newness of each group gives us an occasion again to learn and to belong.

THE SEARCHERS

Searchers, on the other hand, experience a different dilemma. We have had a religious upbringing, or know enough about it to have experienced some form of the life of faith. This religious experience was usually very confusing, abstract, frustrating, or even at times demeaning.

We all know horror stories of early religious experiences, and we say, "Well, they'll just have to get over it," or "They're just rebelling." Both may be true, but neither heals easily. One woman recalls how at age six she was asked to cut out of paper a big, white heart. Then she was to draw big, dark spots on it for each sin she could remember committing. By the time she had finished, the heart was almost all dark spots. Then she was told Jesus' blood cleansed her black heart. Of course, that conclusion was the point of the learning experience, but she failed to comprehend the cleansing part. It was devastating for a six year old exploring her fragile sense of self, and she has never forgotten it. She is indelibly marked and still feels deep anger with the church.

Many people with experiences like this woman become Searchers. As adults we begin to yearn for a deeper meaning in life, a spiritual dimension to life. Many go on a *search* for that dimension but in spiritual, nonreligious groups that offer answers that seem more real, more intellectually feasible, less painful, more rigorous.

We Searchers are avoiding the memories of the simplistic solutions, the ideals, the rigidity, the actual hypocrisy of the religious experience of our youth. We become communities of nonreligious faith seekers. We link up freely with new leaders who look as though they really have found the secret, sound logical and look attractive. An absolutely insatiable desire to have the answer and to be part of a movement is what drives Searchers.

Searchers are on an honest quest and a real journey, but we are wearing a disguise without even consciously knowing it. We cannot for the present admit even to ourselves what we really want, and our spiritual experiences seem to feel the void, perhaps for years. Ultimately, there remains a vacuum underneath it all. But not until the search takes us to the spiritual hinterlands will we finally discover that the search is futile unless taken inside and deeper.

The major difference between people caged at stage 1 and those caged at stage 2 is this: At stage 1 we think we are wrong and weak; others are right and strong. At stage 2 we think we are right and strong; others are wrong and weak.

MOVING FROM STAGE 2 TO STAGE 3

RECOGNIZE UNIQUENESS

The move from the second to the third stage in our journey basically requires us to jump in, concentrate on self-development in the appropriate areas, and take risks in our faith in order to gain enough confidence to participate in the productive life.

This happens in a number of ways. However, we must bring with us a sense of uniqueness. We need to see ourselves as special creatures of God. We gradually recognize that we can make a contribution, regardless of how large or small, that will make a difference. Some circles refer to this as identifying our gifts.

IDENTIFY GIFTS

In order to make valid contributions, it is very important to acknowledge that we have gifts and that they are worthwhile, whatever they are. These are two steps, both of which are vital. We have gifts *and* they are worthwhile. Frequently, we get to the first and fail to reach the second. It is hard to use our gifts in spiritual ways if we cannot see them as being as good as the gifts of others. And if we have leadership gifts, we ought to acknowledge them, whether it fits into our role or not. So many women in particular get stuck between stages 2 and 3 because they have felt devalued and have not been recognized for their gifts (both by themselves and by others).

SEE YOURSELF AS A CONTRIBUTOR

When we move to stage 3, we begin to change our perspective of ourselves and the group. We now see ourselves as contributors to others in leadership, service, ideas, actual products, teaching, counseling, music, instead of viewing ourselves primarily as recipients from others. As we plunge ahead, our scope widens. Our help needed in a pinch turns into a cause; our committee assignment becomes a chairmanship; our writing becomes an article or book; our discussion becomes a talk to the larger community; or our listening becomes counseling.

SEEK RESPONSIBILITY

As this process develops, we begin to like the visibility and added responsibility. We become more confident and are willing to take more risks. We need to know our strengths to do this. Consequently, the transition encourages us to acknowledge and develop our personal gifts and talents to serve our community. We may even pursue this by participating in leadership training or by seeking a special gift. The process is clearly one of building up, feeling good, concentrating on confidence, acknowledging strengths.

THE CRISIS OF MOVEMENT: STAGE 2 TO 3

RISK TAKING

The group at stage 2 becomes such a comfortable place to be and provides so much security that it becomes very difficult to move to a different place, even when supported and urged by the group. We must take risks, deal with uncertainty, volunteer, say yes, try something new, if we are going to grow at this stage. To do that we need continually to develop confidence that we can do it because we have the support from belonging to the community.

ACCEPTANCE OF GIFTS

The second reason we fail to move is an outright denial of the gifts that we have, usually out of fear of using them or having them rejected. What then would we have to acknowledge if we used our gifts? We will have to acknowledge that we are unique, worthwhile in ourselves, responsible, talented. We will have to accept our new confidence and take on a few more battles than perhaps we feel ready to do. We will need perhaps to accept praise and recognition. Every move for us once again acknowledges that we are worthwhile, talented, capable, and loved. It is time to pass it on.

SUMMARY OF STAGE 2:
THE LIFE OF DISCIPLESHIP

Thesis: Faith is learning about God.

Characteristics of Stage 2

Meaning from belonging

Answers Found in a Leader, Cause, or
Belief System

Sense of Rightness

Security in Our Faith

Caged at Stage 2

Rigid in Righteousness, We against Them,
Switchers, Searchers

Moving from Stage 2 to Stage 3

Recognize Uniqueness, Identify Gifts,
Recognize Contributions, Seek Responsibility

Crisis of Movement

Risk Taking, Acceptance of Gifts

Question

When have you felt a part of a faith or spiritual community?

EXPERIENCING STAGE 2

QUESTIONS

1. When have you felt uplifted by a faith or spiritual community?

2. When have you been confused about your spirituality or faith and experienced a group or leader helping you discover the insight or answer you were seeking?

3. Who are the spiritual heroes and heroines that you follow?

EXERCISES

1. Write down the groups to which you belong, including work, family, friendships, community, leisure, and faith groups. List them. Note what major thing, feeling, concrete benefit you get from each one. Ask yourself why you are a member of each. Note what you get that is similar or different from your faith/church groups. How do you feel about your belonging needs being met by your groups?

2. Have a conversation in your journal with someone you follow or think has answers you lack. Ask initial questions like "Who are you?" "What were you trying to tell me?" or "What role do you play in my life?" Let the conversation evolve. What do you hear and learn from this?

3. Read the words of the old hymn "Trust and Obey" and absorb its meaning for you. Can you feel the comforting message, the goodness, the safety if you follow the instruction? Let each verse sink in and then record your reaction to each one.

When we walk with the Lord In the light of His Word
What a glory He sheds on our way!
While we do His goodwill He abides with us still,
And with all who will trust and obey.

Not a shadow can rise, Not a cloud in the skies,
But His smile quickly drives it away;
Not a doubt nor a fear, Not a sigh nor a tear
Can abide while we trust and obey.

Not a burden we bear, Not a sorrow we share,
But our toil He doth richly repay;
Not a grief nor a loss, Not a frown nor a cross
But is blest if we trust and obey.

Refrain: Trust and obey,
for there's no other way
To be happy in Jesus
But to trust and obey.

4. Honestly reveal to yourself what your feelings
   are about your early religious experiences.
   What was good, disappointing, troubling? Ask
   yourself if you want to get relief from the pain
   of it or reexperience the joys of it. Reflect on
   your answer and the feelings it arouses in you.

5

Stage 3:
The Productive Life

"I know what my faith is all about and how great it is for me. I have a strong sense of responsibility to lead others on the same path to fullness in God that I feel. I want so much to share my joy."

"I feel totally self-sufficient when I'm in nature. I feel so strong and at one with the universe. Everything is good. All seems right and I am challenged to accomplish good for others because of the gifts that I've been given."

"I feel called to be a leader. God has gifted me with talents that I want to put to use for others. I love to see people discover their gifts and then use them to further God's plan for this world."

"Now that I've been in AA awhile, I feel the responsibility of being a sponsor to someone else is a high calling that I will accept."

"Everything has been coming together since I've become a Christian. Being successful seems like it goes with being a faithful Christian."

"I never thought I could do it, be in charge of the nursery at church, but I have really accepted God's strength which God gives me for each Sunday."

"I really don't enjoy being in charge, but people keep putting me there. I guess they want me, and God must too. My track record must offer some credibility. I do hope I can continue to do well."

"My purpose in life is to make a difference in the lives of others."

"I used to be a really insecure and needy person. Now I have a sense of security and confidence and feel that my life is going somewhere. Faith is such a confidence builder!"

Stage 3 is best described as the "doing" stage. It is the period of time when we most consciously find ourselves working for God. In fact, our faith is characterized as just that, working for God or being in God's service. Having gone through the apprenticeship period, the life of discipleship, we are ready to go it on our own, even to move on to help others learn to do and be what we have discovered. In fact, this stage is a natural extension of the previous stage. This happens regardless of what kind of background we have had, whether it is conservative, moderate, or liberal. Having been given to and having received so much from our association with others, the time of reciprocity has come. It is now our turn to give in return.

This usually is a very active phase on the critical journey. It is positive and dynamic, centered on being productive in the area of our faith. It nourishes us because it is so personally rewarding, even when the objective is to help others. In helping or leading, we also are fed, so it operates on goals and achievements, building and creating. This can be an unsettling period too, since some people feel pushed into it before they are ready or before they are grounded securely in the previous stage. Others feel pulled into this stage and then do not ever want to leave its magnetic power. Some women, however, find this stage to be very painful stage, if their church discourages them from using their gifts and skills.

The appearance in our life of symbols of the faith we cherish provides one of the primary ways to tell if our faith is working productively. People have cited these signs as ways to recognize faith at work at this particular stage: health, success at work, community service, good family and children, pleasant personal appearance, active participation in church programs, experiencing the gifts of the Spirit (e.g., tongues, healing, Jesus' presence, prophecy), doing good deeds for others, or leading others in the right cause or to a personal faith in Christ.

For many, this stage describes the height of their faith experience. It feels exciting, fulfilling, awesome, inspiring, fruitful. And it usually calls for more effort from us and others. It seems to be almost an insatiable period because everything is going so well. For some, this is captured in the phrase, "if God be for us, who can be against us?"

CHARACTERISTICS OF STAGE 3

UNIQUENESS IN THE COMMUNITY

Because our gifts are unique to each of us, each person can play a different role in the community of faith. Our gifts need to be used. They are given for the common good of the community of faith. By using them we contribute something specific to the community in return for all that we have been given and for the nurturing we have received. It also makes us feel better about ourselves to know that we are special and have special gifts, once we have come to accept that reality. We experience a gradual increase in confidence that precedes the full development of this stage in our lives. At some point, we are able to accept the fact that we can do specific things well. We are skilled and talented and thus have unique value as individuals.

For a time, when we are recognizing, organizing, and putting into practice our special gifts, we appear to be relatively self-centered. We have to look at ourselves to discover which gifts or talents we most want to use and to find out how to use them. On the journey of faith, we accept these as God's gifts to us. We want to use these abilities ultimately to glorify God and to be fully ourselves.

Sometimes people who have worked for a long time at one job or task, either in the community of faith or in other areas, will discover at this stage that they have other talents. Then they will want to make a change. The faith community offers a good place to explore new talents and skills in an accepting and loving environment. Sometimes boredom or fatigue in using our gifts is an inner urge or call to go deeper, to study or learn, to find our own personal ministry in a new way.

Others outside the organized Church can also experience this stage in ways that parallel those within the Church. Using our uniqueness in the group means accepting our talents and skills in any productive way, offering to our own community our spiritual gifts. Leading causes, public speaking, writing, planning strategies, managing others offer prime examples. Some people are adverse to the organized Church but feel they are very ethical or moral in their lives, using their gifts for the good of others. They consider themselves spiritual and on the journey as well.

We actually get our reference to "talents" from a story in the Gospels about three workers who were given "talents" of silver to manage while the landowner was away. Two of the three invested their talents, but the third buried his to protect it from loss or harm (Matt. 25:14–30). In Acts 13:2 there is an illustration of this stage in the early church at Antioch. This group had a number of people who had contributed significantly to their life together. But during one of their worship services, the Holy Spirit asked them to "set apart for me Barnabas and Saul for the work to which I have called them." Thus began the missionary work of Barnabas and Paul. In 1 Cor. 12:8–10, Paul lists "gifts" that are to be used by individuals for the growth and development of the whole community: they include speaking wisely, a knowledgeable word, unusual faith, healing of illnesses, the power to do the incredible, speaking with insight, discernment, speaking in tongues, and the interpretation of tongues.

RESPONSIBILITY

Frequently, the tangible form of productivity at this stage comes in a specific leadership role or in a position within the faith community. We may have served on committees for years and only now have the experience and confidence to speak up more often. Suddenly, we are asked to chair the group! Or we finally agree to teach a Sunday school class, to head up an event, or to lead a youth group, a retreat weekend, or a Bible study. Perhaps it means serving in a special way or representing our church at a gathering of other churches. Maybe we now become a sponsor in our Al-Anon group. Often we do not feel as though we have changed as a person as we take on this responsibility, but we do notice that others are relating to us differently. They perceive us as being more confident and able to take on more.

During this stage, we may also discover the existence of other forms of leadership in the community—forms we would prefer but are not in the traditional vein of those just noted. Everyone has their own form of responsibility with which they are more comfortable, and these are not all publicly visible or recognizable. Perhaps for us, it is raising healthy kids or being available as a surrogate parent to other kids. Or maybe we hold up other people in prayer. Maybe our sense of what is just and ethical in our business dealings sets us apart and gives us a sense of fulfilling our role as one gifted by God. Others use their special talents like singing or giving liberally of their finances. Some see their role in helping those under duress by knitting mittens for the poor, helping the ex-offender find a job, aiding an emigrant family or one who has been the victim of racial prejudice. Maybe our gift is that of being a dear friend or hugging others and letting them know that they are cared for.

Sometimes we come to this responsible role by the loving prodding of someone else who coaxes us into taking on a leadership or productive role that we might not have felt ready for. As we begin to fill that role, we find new strength and talent we did not know were there. This, too, is a gift from God and from the person whose life we touched. It reinforces our sense of doing what is right and being useful. Each of us has an area of responsibility that we can use for God. Our main concern is to be faithful to our task and succeed at it.

The Scriptures are filled with stories about people called by God to perform a special task. The song of Deborah tells the tale of her leadership as judge and deliverer of Israel during a bleak period in her history (Judges 5). The call of Moses represents one of the more dramatic episodes. Alone in the wilderness tending sheep, Moses noticed a "burning bush" only to be confronted by

God, who wanted him to return to Egypt and lead God's people out of their affliction. Moses' birth, miraculous escape from early death in the house of Pharaoh, and then his flight into the wilderness where his wilderness skills were honed for forty years proved to be his special calling. Yet he knew that he was only as capable as his God to accomplish the task. Assured of God's presence and power, Moses returned to lead the Israelites out of Egypt and into the wilderness.

VALUE PLACED ON SYMBOLS

This stage is closely allied with the symbols that represent it: responsibility, authority, recognition, titles, praise from others, influence, respect, allegiance. When we are fruitful, there are rewards, either personally (a job well done, people changed, balanced budget, a spiritual goal reached) or from the community of faith (more responsibility, plaque, thanks, praise). That is not to say there are no complaints. Problems do arise along the way, but we usually overcome them. We are most attracted to the challenge, ego gratification, strengthening of our faith, or the positive recognition that accompanies the responsibility.

The range of symbols for the productive life is broad so we must ask ourselves what, in general, are our significant symbols. For some, just the knowledge that we have done something good, helpful, or in line with the values of our community of faith is enough. It may be satisfaction in doing the right thing or in not doing what is considered to be wrong. The doer feels good, and the recipient of the good or helpful action is grateful as well.

Success in life, regardless of how we define it, represents another outgrowth of faith for some. We may equate our success in life with the strength of our faith, with what we believe. And we draw on our faith in support of our productive lives. For us to be successful means to have been faithful.

Another sign of the productive Christian life for some comes in the explicit gifts of the Spirit. As mentioned earlier, in some traditions the receiving or claiming of special gifts of the Spirit indicates the arrival at this stage in the journey. These gifts enable the gifted person to contribute in a special way to the life of the community. Consider the other abilities like those of apostles, teachers, leaders, and helpers. Others take the fruit of the Spirit as listed in Gal. 5:22–23—love, joy, peace, patience, kindness, goodness, faithfulness, gentleness, self-control—to be the symbols of living the fruitful life.

A SPIRITUAL GOAL REACHED

For some, the form of productivity or fruitfulness may not take on external, visible signs of responsibility, leadership, or success. Rather it may be a sense of having reached a level of spirituality or maturity in the faith that leads to a desire to do something with what has been attained or experienced. Perhaps it is a completion of a seminar, a Bible study, a training period, spiritual direction, a set of spiritual exercises, reaching a new level of giving of our money and/or time. It could be learning to pray in a more meaningful way or simply making it through a major crisis or transition in which God has become very real. Out of that experience, we feel special and able to make our own unique contribution to others.

Whatever the sense of newness or freshness or breadth or depth may be, there is a sense of accomplishment at having come through or prevailed or survived or grown. There is a feeling of some closure, of finishing some leg of the trip or of getting to a milestone. It is a big relief.

No one else can prescribe for us at this stage what will be our source of satisfaction in the acknowledgement of gifts or the reaching of goals. These are ours to discover, create, or acknowledge. That is another reason this stage of fruitfulness is so exciting. We discover what we can be and how we can contribute. We are created by God to be God's resources for others as we discover our own resources.

The Apostle Paul used the metaphor of the long-distance runner in describing his own pursuit of the goal. He wrote somewhat autobiographically in Phil. 3:14 that he "press[es] on toward the goal for the prize of the upward call of God in Christ Jesus." Early in verse 10, he made it clear that his main objective was to "know [Christ] and the power of his resurrection, . . . becoming like him in his death." The experience of knowing Christ in a personal way had made all his previous achievements, notable as they were for his time, of little value.

EXAMPLES OF JOURNEYS AT STAGE 3

Bob: Tending to be an "overachiever" to begin with, I found this stage to be a natural. Eager to learn the ropes and then aware that I had abilities that made me valuable for the particular communities of faith with which I was associated, I have stepped into numerous leadership roles. This stage on the journey began even during my teenage years. At church, I not only was a leader in our youth group but also played the organ for our worship services or led in worship by directing the music and the congregational singing. I even won a national song-leading contest held by a national Christian youth organization, which meant that I was chosen to spend the summer of my junior year with a team of young people touring Venezuela leading youth rallies. Outside the church, I was the president of the our high school Bible club that met weekly. I led singing and even "preached" on occasion in a local youth organization that met regularly on Saturday nights.

The pattern continued with my role changing as I moved into my college years and then into life in the church and in theological education. My sense of spiritual growth was often directly related to how much I was participating in Christian activities, and I judged my effectiveness by the usual standards of my work. This carried over into my studies from undergraduate through graduate levels. As a teacher or professor, the journey was my work. Since it was in theological education, even my work was spiritual.

As a minister on the staff of a large church, my position as teaching minister demanded that I function at this stage. I was no less concerned about the bottom line; how well were we (was I) doing as measured by numbers and levels of involvement. An annual review and the annual report caused me to stop and take inventory to see where we were in relation to where we have been and where we are going. The need to succeed, however, was not so much for my sake as it was a desire to meet the greater need of the community of faith. Subtly I was drawn into feeling that I could and must make a difference.

At the same time, my own spiritual journey seemed to be at a different place. I did not take my spiritual temperature on the basis of how well I was doing my job in ministry. Therefore, where I was personally and where I was as a minister often came into conflict. Naturally, this created a tension in my journey. But I was free to live in one stage and to work and minister in another. It does mean that I take my work seriously but not as the final test of my spirituality.

Suzanne: Several years ago my daughter suffered with anorexia nervosa. As a family we underwent counseling with her, a painful process toward understanding and working to overcome this disease. In the course of her two-year illness, I recall having many lonely and fearful moments when despair threatened to overtake me. There seemed to be few places to which I could turn for affirmation and support at this painful time. I was grateful for the friends who did take the time to listen and to care and for God who was with us on this journey.

In the years following my daughter's slow recovery, I began to receive calls from distraught parents who were seeking a place or a person to which they could turn in their fear and pain. Slowly it became clear to me that a support group was needed that would help others in the way we had been helped. I searched for such a group—both for myself and for others, but I found little that was helpful. I prayed hard about this matter, and I gradually came to believe that God was calling me to this particular task. I found a place to hold a meeting and invited a counselor friend to lead the group. We based the group process on the AA and Al-Anon model. After spreading the word a bit, people began to come. Through the years the group has been a place of support and growth for many, and it has been a tremendous personal and spiritual experience for me.

As parents have sat in that circle week after week and have spoken about their pain and cried their tears and reached out to one another, I have become increasingly aware that God calls us to turn our difficult times into opportunities of growth both for ourselves and for others. Within that circle each week I have experienced the powerful bond of God's healing love. That time together weekly has become, for many of us, almost as important as our weekly worship time at church. People helping people and God at the center of it—that is what it's all about. It has helped me to understand the important spiritual dimension of AA and Al-Anon and why those groups have had such a significant impact on people's lives throughout the years. I feel good to have been used by God in this way, and my own healing has been facilitated by this process. I guess for me the serenity prayer, with which we begin and end our meetings, says it all:

"God, grant me the *serenity* to accept the things I cannot change, the *courage* to change the things I can, and the *wisdom* to know the difference."

CAGED AT STAGE 3

OVERLY ZEALOUS

Some who are stuck at stage 3 make others squirm. We are so zealous and engaging. No one can be around us without hearing our story and our trying to convert them, whether to a charismatic experience, a peace or justice issue, a born-again faith, or the latest spiritual seminar. Hard to fend off, we leave battle scars. We believe so strongly that others need what we have that we cannot rest until we are satisfied that they want it too.

This characteristic does not describe those whose enthusiastic experience in faith compels them to share the joy and life with another or of one who wants others to experience the faith as they have come to know it. Rather, when we are caged at this stage, we insist on personal acceptance of and participation in our experience because that makes us feel successful in our faith. We take personal satisfaction in having saved others from some horrible fate. They can become productive like we are, and we can get the credit.

WEARY IN WELL DOING

Perhaps you have heard the phrase or seen it on t-shirts, "Shop until you drop." Humorous but telling. The same idea describes us when caged here. We work so hard at whatever we are doing as part of our faith experience that we become weary in well doing. We are burning out and frequently at the same time feeling unappreciated without knowing why. People did not change in the ways we wanted them to or at the pace we expected. Or we feel our leadership does not result in the breakthroughs we desired from it. Usually the complaint boils down to one thing. Others disappointed us. Usually, someone else is at fault. We tried as hard as we could to "make it happen." So we are very disappointed, sometimes even bitter.

SELF-CENTERED

The more successful we are at stage 3, or the more productive we become, the more tempting it is to slip into the cage of self-centeredness, even self-worship. We feel indispensable to the group. "No one else could do it better because my gifts and abilities are so well suited for this position." We are devastated if not chosen for obvious assignments. We enjoy the feelings of others rallying around us because it compensates for our unconscious insecurities and balances our unacknowledged fears. We try to do it all, by ourselves, even though it is God's work.

Feeling almost invincible we are led in lock-step progression to playing God again in our own life and in the lives of others. There is a subtle feeling when caged at this stage of being given success because of being and/or doing good. The harder we work, the more success we have, the stronger our faith must be. We put our desires in the place of God and call it God's will. And if challenged we will deny it vehemently, frequently using Scripture or other evidence to prove us right. We can parry the challenge by attributing jealousy or immaturity to the challengers.

LIFE AS PERFORMANCE

Life becomes a performance, an act, a play, a drama in which we are the leading persons and all goes well. We cannot be vulnerable or look weak in front of others because we would be out of control. We are angry at God inside and very fearful of being found out, so our facade is stronger than ever. We look almost perfect to those around us. We are frequently worshiped as heroes. We thrive on the audience reaction. Their applause becomes addictive. We go back for more and more. We strive so hard to be loved for what we have done rather than for who we are. We are ultimately very, very lonely people.

MOVING FROM STAGE 3 TO STAGE 4

LOSE SENSE OF CERTAINTY

This transition becomes very difficult because the certainty of stage 3 dissolves into uncertainty and questioning at stage 4. There are several key experiences in this transition. First, we let the questions come instead of denying them. Then we seek support, even though the process is quite solitary. We walk the fine line between searching out answers and resting in God for the answers.

EXPERIENCE FAITH/PERSONAL CRISIS

This move from stage 3 to 4 is most likely precipitated by a crisis in our life or our faith. That crisis makes many of the former truths and answers inadequate or inappropriate for the next phase in the journey. It often initiates a slow, deep, anguishing questioning of our faith, our relationship with God. We have no answers, just blank pages. We begin to search for ways to resolve our faith dilemmas.

FEEL ABANDONED

There may even be a time in which we sense the loss of God. God appears to have abandoned us, disappeared without a trace. Losing the certainty and reality of God, we do not know yet how to ask or where to turn in the darkness. We feel overwhelmed. This is clearly the most alarming place of all the journey. While the doubts or crises are there, we frequently feel as though God is not there when we need God most. This, however, may be part of the transition for many of us. It sets the stage for the inevitable, humbling, crumbling experience of re-discovering God again.

LOOK FOR DIRECTION

Our faith, our relationship with God, must change before it can be remolded. This is natural, although frightening, for most of us, because it rocks some of the foundations we've been relying upon, maybe since childhood. In the transition to stage 4, we can be assisted by many fellow pilgrims on the journey, people who are experiencing what we are, or who already have and are not afraid of the doubts and uncertainties. At stage 4, very little feels certain, especially at first.

* * *

This is a good place to reiterate that the stages on the journey of faith are fluid and not so clearly defined in real life as we have set them down here. We move back and forth from day to day and may be in all three of the stages we've described simultaneously. But there may be, in the stages mentioned, one that seems to fit best and most realistically for you now, at this point in your life, one that you keep returning to for its closeness to your heart. Keep that stage in mind as we continue to describe the rest of the journey.

CRISIS OF MOVEMENT FROM STAGE 3 TO STAGE 4

LETTING GO OF SUCCESS

The accomplishments and success at stage 3 are very gratifying. We feel confident, competent, well respected, liked. We really don't want to face the clouds of uncertainty at stage 4. So it is difficult to voluntarily move into this transition. We usually sense we have already started to lose something we cherish, or what we cherish does not give us what we want as it once did. Grief usually accompanies the transition from stage 3 to stage 4.

ACCEPTING VULNERABILITY

We know at some less conscious level that we are moving into an area of uncertainty, loss, confusion, perhaps bleakness. We feel more loss than gain. It is very difficult to strip spiritually before God and come to terms with spiritual integrity. We cannot flee from God but are called face to face with God, and that may make us more vulnerable than we have ever been before. Unless we are willing to lean into these fears, we will likely move to stages 2 or 3 where that vulnerability is reduced and security is more readily available.

SUMMARY OF STAGE 3:
THE PRODUCTIVE LIFE
Thesis: Faith is working for God.

Characteristics of Stage 3
Uniqueness in the Community
Responsibility
Value Placed on Symbols
A Spiritual Goal Reached

Caged at Stage 3
Overly Zealous, Weary in Well Doing,
Self-Centered, Life as Performance

Moving from Stage 3 to Stage 4
Lose Sense of Certainty, Experience Faith/
Personal Crisis, Feel Abandoned, Look for Direction

Crisis of Movement
Letting Go of Success, Accepting Vulnerability

Question
Which of your talents/gifts do you feel
good about and are willing to share?

EXPERIENCING THIS STAGE

QUESTIONS

1. Which of your talents or gifts do you feel good about and are willing to use?
2. When have you accepted a spiritual responsibility in a community (work, home, city)?
3. Are you working on any particular spiritual goals?

EXERCISES

1. Have you ever been so thrilled with events or with something you did that you wanted to shout or cry or run or do a soft-shoe shuffle right there in front of everybody? Remember King David? He was so excited when the Ark of the Covenant (place of God's presence in Israel) finally was being brought back into the Holy City that he "danced before the Lord with all his might" (2 Sam. 6:14). The next time you feel enthusiastic about something, remember that that word means literally "God within" you. So let God be God within you and do not be afraid to express God's presence. Read the following poem, and let your own sense of being unique sink into your heart and then be expressed.

God Danced
On the day I was born, God danced.
Did you really, God?
Was it a ritualistic, dignified,
bow-from-the-waist kind of dance?
Or was it just possibly a wild and crazy
arm-flinging kind of thing?

Did you pronounce somberly
that here was another 'good girl'
that you had created?

Or did you yell and holler and
grab the guy on the corner
to let him know that this time
you had really done it!
This time you created a winner—
This one was going to go all the way!

I hope you did, God—
I really hope you did.

Sarah Hall Maney

2. Turn to Exod. 3:1–4:17 and slowly read about God's call to Moses to use his gifts of leadership. Can you empathize with his reluctance and then his obedient response to God's leading? Are there areas in your life where you are called to lead and may feel reluctant? Can you bring those fears and hesitations openly to God to let them be transformed?

3. Occasionally we need to take our spiritual temperature. It can tell us how we are experiencing the richness of the faith. One simple way to check is to list the fruits of the Spirit and ask which we are experiencing and in what amount. Use the list on the following page to note where you feel strong, neutral, or weak.

	Strong	Neutral	Weak
Love	_____	_____	_____
Joy	_____	_____	_____
Peace	_____	_____	_____
Patience	_____	_____	_____
Kindness	_____	_____	_____
Goodness	_____	_____	_____
Faithfulness	_____	_____	_____
Gentleness	_____	_____	_____
Self-control	_____	_____	_____

Take to God those areas in which you sense a need for help, or for renewal.

6

Stage 4:
The Journey Inward

"I have this old saying that fits right now. 'Just when I got it all together, I forgot where I put it!' That's how I feel about my spiritual life."

"There must be other ways of being spiritual that are even more satisfying than this and will heighten my sense of God-likeness. I'm going to search for them."

"This time in my life feels the most desolate imaginable. I am so estranged from God, from my faith, from life—I'm not sure even how to proceed. I feel like melting away."

"I can no longer go on basing my faith on what's right for others or what feels good. I must find out once and for all what God's truth is for me in my own life. But how do I go about that?"

"How can I be in a leadership position and have such deep doubts about so much of my faith? I feel like a real hypocrite."

"Every inch of the journey these days is excruciating. One revelation after another, discovering things I'd stuffed away twenty-five years ago and never wanted to look at again."

"I've never really known who God was for me before this time. I finally know in my soul what it means to let God be God."

"Now I know the true meaning of 'pride goeth before a fall.' I certainly fell!"

"I never knew what spiritual self-esteem was until I found my honest self in God. I'm a different person. I'm well, and becoming a whole person."

Stage 4, The Journey Inward, is aptly described by its title, for it is a deep and very personal inward journey. It almost always comes as an unsettling experience yet results in healing for those who continue through it. Until now, our journey has had an external dimension to it. Our life of faith was more visible, more outwardly oriented, even though things certainly were happening inside us. But the focus fell more on the outside, the community of faith, nature, leadership, the display and use of the Spirit's gifts, belonging, and productivity.

At this stage, we face an abrupt change (at least many do) to almost the opposite mode. It's a mode of questioning, exploring, falling apart, doubting, dancing around the real issues, sinking in uncertainty, and indulging in a self-centeredness. We often look hopeless to those around us.

A symbolic name for people in this stage is the "vertical people." It is a time when the issues go primarily up and down between you and God. Others are involved, but the focus is on the issues, battle, healing, and resolution in your relationship with God.

It becomes painfully clear, after some initial squirming in another attempt to be comfortable, that the right direction, rather than right answers have to come from God. That realization generally comes through a deep inner journey; one that we are not informed or taught about and for which there are few models available. Somewhere toward the end of stage 4 we experience the Wall; a face-to-face experience with God and with our own will. This is such a critical experience that we have devoted all of chapter 7 to it.

It would be great to think that most priests, ministers, and other spiritual leaders could be our guides through stage 4 and the Wall. The sad truth is that many of these leaders have not been led through this stage themselves and have not allowed themselves to question deeply or to become whole. So many of those to whom we often look most naturally for help are inadequate guides for this part of the journey. Those who have been through this stage themselves and may be specially trained in spiritual direction, spiritual formation, or pastoral counseling are unique people and are to be sought out.

CHARACTERISTICS OF STAGE 4

LIFE OR FAITH CRISIS

Most of us are so comfortable and self-sufficient at the previous stage (called the productive or fruitful life) that we have no natural tendency to move at all. In fact, stage 4 does not even look like part of the journey for those of us at home in stage 3. It does not appear to be an extension of our faith and growth. Consequently, we are not drawn in this direction. When this stage comes, many feel propelled into it by an event outside themselves. It's usually a crisis that turns their world upside down.

If we have been people of strong faith, our life, though not necessarily easy, has fit nicely into our faith framework. Then the event or crisis often takes on major proportions. It often strikes close to our core, for example, our children, spouse, work, or health. For the first time, our faith does not seem to work. We feel remote, immobilized, unsuccessful, hurt, ashamed, or reprehensible. Neither our faith nor God provides what we need to soothe us, heal us, answer our prayers, fulfill our wishes, change our circumstances, or solve our problems. Our formula of faith, whatever that may have been, does not work any more, or so it appears. We are stumped, hurting, angry, betrayed, abandoned, unheard, or unloved. Many simply want to give up. Their life of faith may even seem to have been a fraud at worst, a mirage at best.

Some enter this stage of the journey through a crisis in their faith more than in their personal lives. This is particularly true for people raised in churches with a clearly defined belief system, one with a strong code of conduct that provided guidance and answers for life and life's questions. For many in this tradition, the journey from the initial stage to stage 3 follows a fairly straightforward, smooth course.

Suddenly, something in one's strict adherence is called into question. One of the foundation blocks crumbles. Perhaps someone considered to be a model of faith, a person of genuine piety, is exposed for being involved in an immoral or illegal activity. Perhaps another way of looking at the Scriptures or relating to God and life begins to catch one's attention. For example, specific doctrines about Scripture or the Church's infallibility come into question. Gnawing questions become more and more unmanageable, questions about what we believe and have believed and about how we live and why we do and do not do certain things. We are no longer able to ignore or repress them. They haunt us continually. So much so that we become aware of a larger gap in our lives of faith. We sense ourselves slipping more and more into a period of limbo.

In the Scriptures, Peter's life may best illustrate how crisis throws everything out of kilter. He had left family, home, and business to follow Jesus (Mark 1:16–18; 10:28). In front of Jesus and all his friends, he came with assurance to confess Jesus to be the expected Messiah (Mark 8:29). Suddenly, on Good Friday, the answers did not fit. So certain had he and his friends been of who Jesus was and what Jesus was to do in Jerusalem that they could not comprehend those warnings about pending disaster. But the arrest of Jesus placed in jeopardy all of Peter's beliefs about what God was doing in Jesus. Disappointed, confused, and maybe even a little angry, Peter abandoned his friend and then denied any knowledge of Jesus (Mark 14:66–72). His tears reflected his brokenness. The Peter who emerged after Easter to lead the Church after Pentecost was a different Peter from the man for whom the cock had crowed.

LOSS OF CERTAINTIES IN LIFE AND FAITH

At stage 3, The Productive Life, so many things seem to be true, certain, and successful. Then things begin to unravel, and some people find themselves asking a lot of questions about themselves, doubting the full emergence of their selves. This insatiable appetite for more growth and development of meaning is especially true for those with intellectual curiosity, for those with education as a strong value in their background. We have experienced much spiritual insight by arriving at new levels of self-actualization. We think we should now go beyond the teachings and reach for new heights. At least we feel we should broaden ourselves to obtain the wisdom of many more spiritual leaders or ideas. We have become more convinced that there is spiritual perfection, but we do not know which way is correct. We are confused by so many logical approaches to spirituality. So we search, adding each new experience to all the others, increasing our vocabulary and practicing more spiritual rites and exercises.

Many of us intellectual searchers are careful to separate the spiritual from the religious because we have found a true way outside of traditional organized religion. At stage 4, we have become confused in our search for inner meaning and purpose. Our pain comes from a paradox. We look outside ourselves for ways to have more inner control. Inner control brings about more confusion and pain. Our inner hunger is increasing at the same time we are beginning to doubt the very core of our belief in self-actualization. We become aware of a vague uneasiness and an increase in the momentum or drama of the search for self.

One might look to the disciples on the road to Emmaus in Luke 24:13–35 as an example of this stage. Unknown to us by name, these two disciples apparently were leaving Jerusalem on the way to Emmaus after the events of Good Friday when they were joined by a stranger. When asked about their conversation, the two disciples stopped and, with great sadness, asked if the stranger was the only visitor in Jerusalem who did not know what had happened in the past few days. They then related the story of Jesus, his surprising death, and the confusing word about the empty tomb. Nothing made sense any more. The story was not ending as they thought it would. It had all fallen apart on them. They were left confused and puzzled.

A SEARCH FOR DIRECTION, NOT ANSWERS

The answers, such as being in control or being spiritually powerful, now have a hollow ring for many in this stage. We crave something more personal, more fulfilling. The "God-shaped vacuum" of the French philosopher Pascal now has been recognized, but there is confusion as to how to fill it. To get to the stage of productive living, we had learned things like obedience, innocence, belonging, and being in the center. They no longer serve us, and we begin slowly to change our approach to God. We move from a posture of knowing to one of seeking. At this stage, all we can say is that we are seeking a direction so vague and unclear that it is frightening. We know that we are no longer seeking *an* answer.

This dealing with uncertainty also moves us to a more personal level. We are seeking deep inner direction for our lives. We want peace in our brokenness. Perhaps it's the search for healing, a deep psychological and spiritual healing. Or it is the search for life's meaning that goes deeper and is more service oriented. It could be coming to terms with ourselves, with God, and with others. Although it represents a long journey, we find ourselves longing for it. As one person put it, "My life was going along well, but it felt so flat, as if I would never get any deeper. So I went for help; not for a specific problem but for a dis-ease of the soul."

The biblical story of Job is a classic case of one who had more answers from his so-called comforters than he could handle. But they did not address his experience. He needed direction rather than the usual answers, which no longer seemed to fit reality. In his physical and spiritual agony, Job sought direction from his God whom he had trusted and in whom he continued to trust despite his questions.

PURSUIT OF PERSONAL INTEGRITY IN
RELATION TO GOD

Stage 4 allows us, invites us, and compels us to know ourselves and to know God in all God's fullness. We may experience a complete turnabout in our concept of both ourselves and God. This often comes through a slow process. It is a process of pursuing our integrity or discovering who we are as opposed to who others want us to be. This is a strenuous and courageous process. At the next stage, we find out who God wants us to be, and that is even more profound than who we think we are.

The deeper search at this stage can be lonely, and that often leads to frustration. The people who desperately want security and solace will stop the pursuit temporarily or will get stuck at this stage in the journey. Consequently, there are fewer travelers among the number of people who have come to this stage in the journey.

In stage 4, the answers are replaced by questions. The journey is intensely personal and difficult to share with others. That makes it hard to develop any sense of belonging. The haunting doubts themselves cause additional alienation from others and lead us to feel at times as though we were the ones in the wrong, the bad persons, or the ones with the weak faith. When our family and/or friends seem *so* sure, we are so very unsure. We cannot look at our spiritual needs at this stage without eventually including our whole selves, because our spirituality becomes our whole selves as we proceed. Our pain may well extend to mental and emotional as well as to spiritual anguish. It means giving up a lot of our well-worn defenses and becoming extremely vulnerable.

The psalmists often wrote of their search for integrity before God. One of the best-known passages comes from Ps. 139:23–24: "Search me, O God, and know my heart! Try me and know my thoughts! And see if there be any wicked way in me, and lead me in the way everlasting!"

GOD RELEASED FROM BOX

At this stage we discover painfully that God is not who we had thought God was. God is very different. Instead of having had God pretty well figured out and having accepted or rejected others' views of God, we now have to contend with a God who is much more personally available to us. It does not feel this way during the dark period of this stage (when confronting the Wall), but eventually, we come to see that we had placed God in a box

—a box of our own making, perhaps constructed in our child-hood. We had prescribed who God was for ourselves and for others. Now God breaks out of the box. God no longer repre-sents our own worn out or frightening father, brother, savior, or warrior images. God takes on new, healing, and personal images that expand our view of God's presence. At the same time, these images personalize that presence in a profound way.

But we fight against the change in images. We have a lot at stake to keep God where we are most comfortable. If we had a brutal father or an absent one and, therefore, cannot relate to God as father, we have to experience healing and forgive our own fathers before we can redeem or heal the old image of God as father. So we come to a roadblock. For a time, it is easier to blame the Church, God, or our parents for this spiritual impasse than it is to come to terms with the pain of abandonment, to understand and feel our anger, and to forgive our own fathers in order to reclaim the powerfully healing image of God as a caring father. The same resistance holds true for the image of God as mother, because so many of us have not allowed the wounded relationships with our own mothers to heal.

The story of Jonah illustrates a person who has God in a box. Not wanting to accept the fact that his God could care for people different from his type, Jonah jumped ship to avoid adapting. Unfortunately, his flight from reality nearly cost him his life. Faced again with the alternatives, Jonah decided to accept the fact, in theory at least, that God knew neither national or racial boundaries. When the people of Nineveh turned to God, Jonah began to pout because what he had feared had come true. The story ends with him angry at God because God had indeed been gracious with the detestable people of Nineveh. Jonah's anger was so intense that he wished he could die. He was much more comfortable with a provincial view of God who played favorites.

APPARENT LOSS OF FAITH

One of the most difficult aspects of this stage in the journey lies in the sense gained from ourselves and others that we really are losing our faith and being disloyal to the group, the church, the organization, the leader, ourselves and our beliefs. Epithets like "selling out," "giving in," "weak," "wrong," or "misguided" suddenly come our way. This sensation does not belong exclusively to the more conservative types who, for example, might question one who participates in a much broader ecumenical setting. It occurs in even the most liberal organizations when the liberal person begins to make arbitrary distinctions and commitments. It even happens in the nonchurch spirituality groups, when a New Age or an Eastern thinker questions human perfection and accepts sinfulness and forgiveness. Moving away from collective beliefs or a belief system brings discomfort and, frequently, tension, which leads to a break with that group or community. This, too, adds to the loneliness by making us alone in a lonely process.

The Elijah story of 1 Kings 18–19 graphically illustrates the pattern of one who had moved into stage 4. As punishment for Israel's worship of Baal under the influence of wicked King Ahab and his wife Jezebel, it had not rained for three years. Then Elijah, God's prophet, challenged the prophets of Baal to a showdown on Mount Carmel. All morning the prophets of Baal made futile attempts to call forth a response from their god. Elijah, who had rebuilt the altar of the Lord Yahweh, ordered his offering and altar soaked with four pitchers of water three different times. He prayed to God, who sent fire from heaven, which consumed the offering, the altar (wood, stones, dirt, and all) and the water in the surrounding trench. Elijah was at the height of his "success" stage.

Unfortunately, Jezebel was not impressed. She put a price on Elijah's head, which created a major personal and faith crisis for him. He was afraid and fled for his life into the wilderness. Depressed, he sat under a small tree and prayed. So deep was his despair that he wished to die. Instead he went to sleep. An angel awoke him, and told him to get up and eat the food prepared for him. Elijah did so but immediately went back to sleep. The angel came a second time, fed him, and told him to get up and get moving—to take a forty-day trip to Mount Horeb. Note the classic symptoms of fear followed by flight, depression, a death wish, exhaustion, sleep and more sleep, and finally by a directive from someone to get moving.

Elijah obeyed and at Horeb (called the "Mountain of God") entered a cave, a fitting place for one in deep depression. God then came to Elijah and asked him to examine himself, to ask what was going on in his life and why he was where he was. Elijah replied in self-pity, whining that he had worked zealously for God only to have Israel reject God and kill the prophets. "I, even I only, am left; and they seek my life, to take it away." He conveniently had forgotten all that had succeeded up to that point. Life seemed now to have lost any relevance. Even God seemed so remote that Elijah had not bothered to get in touch. He felt utterly alone (forgetting the hundreds like him who also were hiding in caves and who had not bowed to Baal)!

EXAMPLES OF SPIRITUAL JOURNEYS AT STAGE 4

Stephen: I spent my first eighteen years, as the older of two children, in a town of seven thousand people where there was trust and lots of affirmation, since everyone knew each other. I viewed life as good, caring, and whole. In most ways, I felt special and valuable. Though church was not an important part of my family's life, I was taught to pray and taken to Sunday school as a child. However, my memories of early religious experiences have little or nothing to do with the organized church. My parents taught me the Lord's Prayer when, as a small child, I had the chicken pox. I remember my father, especially, taking the time to teach me that prayer.

I grew up believing that there was a God who created the world and who, if I lived a good life, was caring and willing to provide good things for me. My first real contemplation of God came as an elementary school child. I was lying in my backyard on a warm summer night looking at the stars. I had heard in school that the universe was infinite, so I asserted intellectually that something must have started it all and put it in place. That something would be God.

My own conversion experience came as a college freshman during football season. A young man came into our room and witnessed to us using a booklet containing four spiritual laws. He asked me if I had ever committed my life to Christ as a personal Lord and Savior. I was offended by the self-righteous and aggressive style and promptly kicked him out of our room in an obscene way. Then I asked my roommate what he thought about this since he claimed to be religious. He said he did not like the style but thought the question about knowing God personally through Jesus Christ was an excellent question.

I remember offering my life to Jesus by simply stating that, if he were personal and did love me and wanted to be with me, then I wanted that relationship too. My conversion was not dramatic or traditional in the sense of involving repentance of my own sinfulness. It was more a personal awareness of being incomplete and a desire to be whole.

My college behavior would appear to be schizophrenic, or at least immoral to many Christians! I was deeply involved in the sexual and chemical activities of the sixties. At the same time, I was involved in a personal and growing relationship with Christ and felt a desire to serve and do ministry in a community of faith. A lot of nurture came through this ministry. It was this combination of service and a community of faith that planted the seed for considering the ordained ministry as a vocation.

After graduation I taught for a year. I then began grad school with two options: master's work in physical education, with the hope of college coaching, or pursuit of seminary education. The idea of seminary came after a very dry experience in the faith, which ended in my being drawn back into the Scriptures.

The vocation of ministry has been filled with emotional ups and downs. I have experienced personal success and dry spells along the way, which caused me to question the faith and my choice of vocation. Desert experiences that produce growth are part of my spiritual development. It is a time to rethink and readjust to where God is leading me.

As I have gotten older, I have seen a narrowing of my own personal focus and ministry. I have gained experience and know much of what I personally can or cannot do, where the growth for me is, and the places where I'm limited. In making decisions currently I have asked not where I am to be or what I am to do, but what it is that God is calling me to become.

Much of my life has been a pushing, impatient one of trying to "do things right" instead of waiting for the timing of God and being committed to "doing right things." Such a journey, though I'm aware of its validity, is difficult as I continue to push and move things on my own rather than trust myself and my work to the Creator.

I see my journey as calling me to become more constrained and focused in terms of gifts and use of personal energies and skills. Many of the legalistic and narrow forms of spirituality, which I rebelled against in the past, have come to be part of my life. The goodness of my life spiritually might be summed up in the title of Edna Hong's book *The Downward Ascent*. As I have acknowledged and accepted the strengths and limitations of my self, I have found power to change and accept my life. I'm also now experiencing life more fully and completely. I look forward to this "downward ascent," and I'm willing to endure the joy and pain which it brings.

Mary Lou: God and I became acquainted when I was a child, and we had frequent talks together. As a girl from a staunch religious tradition, I saw God as a master and, especially in my young adult years, a master I must please. Yet as my spiritual life deepened, God became a good friend, someone I talked with on a regular basis about everything.

My one certainty in life was my occupation as a career counselor. It was my purpose in life, my calling. I recall attending a seminar once where someone put into words exactly how I felt about my work. My calling was affirmed for me again. I was doing what I needed to do with my life. I remember the tears of joy at the "knowing." I was comfortable in my work and in my life.

Then the tiredness started. I sought a medical explanation. All the tests proved negative. The conclusion was: "80 percent of all tiredness is stress related."

So I cut back on the number of clients I was seeing. Paradoxically, I felt energized when I was with a client. But running a private practice and doing the preparation work for speeches and seminars left me exhausted. I turned more and more of my work over to my colleagues.

The questions of how to keep a business and how to do my work chased each other around in my head. Was God taking away from me what I liked to do? What I was so sure was my life's purpose?

My tiredness increased. I tried to get more rest. I avoided activities. I isolated myself. I even questioned my intelligence, my skills, my emotional stability. What was I doing to make me feel so tired? What could I do to get out of this quicksand?

Things simply got worse. The more tired I became, the more I began to wonder whether indeed I was good at what I did anyway. Maybe I just needed to quit.

I had experienced darkness, confusion, and emotional pain before, but there had always been some glimmer of light, enough to give me hope. This was different. The darkness, confusion, and pain seemed to totally surround me—invasive, nagging, and energy draining. It just wouldn't go away.

Surprisingly, I didn't have difficulty being in God's presence. My problem was in being present for God. The darkness, confusion, and pain handicapped me. In a monologue, I simply reported my physical tiredness and my state to God.

I took as much time off as possible during the spring and summer and returned to a regular schedule in the fall. Just before I was to give a major speech that fall, I was walking along a trail around a small lake and going through my usual litany with God. As I concluded my monologue, I added that I would appreciate help in getting through the speech. Then I sat down on a bench to rest. Suddenly I was aware of all the sounds of nature. But beyond that and for the first time, I was astonished that each sound was in harmony with all the other sounds.

I desperately wanted to be in tune again, to be able to be in harmony with my friends, my daily work, my business.

And I said out loud, "I can't do this anymore. I'm too tired. I feel as though I need some trauma in my life, whether physical or emotional. I need something to happen so the doctors will believe me!"

I sat for a long time quietly. The monologue was over. I felt God's presence, and his presence surrounded me. Everything was in tune. God had answered me. I simply had to wait.

I gave the speech. It was hardly a great performance, but I got through it. That night I went out with some friends to a new shopping mall. Once again I couldn't keep up with them. I hurried home and went to bed at 10 P.M. Then, at 1:15 in the morning I awoke out of a sound sleep. My heart was beating so fast and so erratically, I couldn't count the beats. I remember laughing and thinking, "Ask and you shall receive." And I thanked God for the answer, asked God to stay with me, and dialed 911. I had my trauma!

CAGED AT STAGE 4

ALWAYS QUESTIONING

Some people caged at stage 4 are never satisfied. We are ever learning, never coming to truth. We always have another question to ask. We are not quite sure we have enough information to let us really commit to the process of restoration or healing. We always have a lingering doubt whether this is the right path or the real truth. We are insatiable learners in the faith, trying every possible road to greater insights. We go to every spiritual growth experience available. We are up on the latest seminars. We appear to be very open on the surface, true seekers of the truth. But we are closed off just below the surface. We are simply afraid to let go and expose ourselves. The risk is too high.

CONSUMED BY SELF-ASSESSMENT

Others caged at this stage are consumed with finding self, not with finding faith. Often we try personal growth just to know ourselves better. But we remain closed. We just want to know things about ourselves that would make us better, more positive, more insightful, but which do not require us to give up our will and be changed. We are unwilling to experience the shadow side of ourselves. We are unwilling to rediscover God.

Some of us want the answer to be less difficult, less personally confronting. We seek something we can reason through instead of feel, or we seek something we can feel instead of reason through. We want God to be personal growth. Indeed, we make a god of personal growth and worship it. Self-growth can be addictive. We replace God with idols of self, even when on the surface it may appear that we are giving up self and finding wholeness. It is an insipid disease.

IMMOBILIZED

People get stuck at this stage because of a lack of or loss of intimacy, with self and others. We feel we are on this journey by ourselves. We can learn from others, even be in groups together, but we cannot connect fully with them for fear of being found out. We cannot reach inward and are unable to reach outward. We are immobilized. Sometimes we are unable to reach inside to do the work of healing necessary to move with God. We may have been so hurt in childhood, by the Church, in a marriage, or by family that we are numb. We cannot feel because feeling would be too painful. Now at stage 4, when asked to journey inward, we may even want to be healed, but we think it cannot happen to us. The risk of looking inside is too great. So we sit and stew. We may experience physical ailments that have a metaphoric character. God is calling, and we are facing a choice. It is a critical juncture, and we are stuck.

It is easy when caged at this stage to revert to some earlier stage. Our discomfort makes us long for a more friendly or familiar surrounding. Frequently, we find the unknown at this stage to be very difficult. If stuck, the journey begins to go in circles. No answer is the right answer. Yet, at this precise moment, a breakthrough is possible. We can admit to God that we are ready to give up trying to find a way out. We can lean into our fears. Instead, we may choose to go back rather than to go on. Finding the unknown too dark or threatening, we lack the courage of faith. So we go to stage 1, a simple faith, or to stage

2, to share the faith of others, or to stage 3, secure in working at it all.

Sometimes people drop off the journey totally at this point. Overwhelmed by pain or crises in our lives, we absolutely cut ourselves off from God. We repudiate the way. It is tragic and sad, but possible. Of course, God is always there with open arms to welcome us back to the journey. But, being so frightened or disillusioned by life's events, we may shut God out completely.

MOVING FROM STAGE 4 TO STAGE 5

LET GO OF SPIRITUAL EGO
(SELF-CENTEREDNESS)

Emerging through the Wall represents the transition to stage 5. We experience a new kind of yielding. We yield at a much deeper level. We relinquish our ego. Essentially it means moving into healing and wholeness, and from there to obedience to God in our life commitments. These life commitments emerge from our new sense of wholeness and God's love. This movement brings us face to face with the God we have rediscovered. We are on our way to more complete healing, which entails a deeper awareness of our weaknesses. We can hear, see, touch, and smell the God of our salvation. We are becoming intimate with God in the fullest sense of the word *intimate.*

ACCEPT GOD'S PURPOSE FOR OUR LIVES

Whereas before we were more confident in ourselves, now we are becoming deeply confident in God to take care of us totally. This transition positions us to let God work God's purposes in us. God finds in us a willing vessel from which love can be offered. We must be aware of ego-centeredness and self-confidence and not be diverted by them. We need to learn to befriend them, laugh at them, and bring them to God.

SEEK WHOLENESS THROUGH PERSONAL
HEALING AND PILGRIMAGE

We are more aware than ever of our creatureliness and faults but less vulnerable to being crippled by those faults. The ongoing, lifelong desire for personal wholeness and healing finds its fullest expression in this transition. We know that God is there. We no longer need to hold on to our needs of the past. We have experienced letting go of some of life's stabilizers at the previous stage. Now letting go is a daily, even hourly, event rather than a one-shot deal. Our personal pilgrimage to a love-centered life begins in earnest, but, most likely, it does not come according to our timing.

BE WILLING TO COMMIT TO WHATEVER IT TAKES

Gradually we feel God's hand fully extending into our lives. Without weighing the facts or seeking alternatives, we give up control of our lives. We commit to whatever God has ahead for us. The experience of God's hand in our lives is so extraordinary that it almost propels us on into this stage. We have begun to trust God, to let God be God in a new way. Out of this trust comes a letting go of anxieties about ourselves such as whether or not we are ready, able, secure, recognized sufficiently, etc. We are more accepting of our brokenness because we are willing to let God use us in ways *God* chooses rather than ways we choose. We become clay in the Potter's hands.

CRISIS OF MOVEMENT FROM STAGE 4 TO STAGE 5

FINDING PEACE THROUGH GIVING UP THE SEARCH FOR SELF

One of the primary issues we face and must deal with in moving to stage 5 is our insatiable hunger to continue searching for self. It appears so good, so wholesome, so useful we may not even notice it as a lure away from God. There is a necessity to search for self at earlier stages. In this transition, however, we are being asked to be selfless and to let go of the search for self, except as it is continually revealed to us by God in the stuff of our lives. It feels like we are asked to give up such a good thing. Yet it is only if we can do this paradoxical thing, give up the search for self to find ourselves in God, that we can find peace. We gradually will be moved to a place in stages 5 and 6 in which we are incapable of doing anything by our own efforts. We are becoming totally dependent on God—as we seemed to be when we began the journey. We once again tap into these same truths.

ALLOWING FOR NEW CERTAINTY IN GOD

Some of us at stage 4 get so used to ambiguity and lack of direction spiritually that we think this is as it should be. We get comfortable not knowing and wandering. We begin to like the search for its own sake. Again, in this transition, we are asked to lean into our fears. In this case, our fear may be that we have to be certain about God, and that God is calling us to stop dancing in front of the Wall.

OPEN TO THE COST OF OBEDIENCE

It is probable that most people shrink back because they begin to understand that God truly will fulfill the promise of transformation in stage 5. Life will never be the same to those of us who are willing to surrender our brokenness—to those being healed, allowing our weaknesses to be available to and used by God. It may seem impossible to see ourselves really being used effectively, or it may seem like too much to ask of us now that our lives are so well established and we have responsibilities to cover. We thought the journey led to healing. We didn't think we'd be invited to suffer. It doesn't seem to be moving in the direction we'd assumed it would. That alone is a good clue that we are still on the journey at this stage—when the obvious is not in the plan.
Once again we are asked to suspend our judgment, to trust even more deeply in our new relationship with God, and to continue the work of surrender as part of the transformation process.

Summary of Stage 4:
The Journey Inward
Thesis: Faith is rediscovering God.

Characteristics
Life or Faith Crisis
Loss of Certainties in Life and Faith
A Search for Direction, Not Answers
Pursuit of Personal Integrity in Relation to God
God Released from Box
Apparent Loss of Faith

Caged at Stage 4
Always Questioning
Consumed by Self-Assessment
Immobilized

Moving from Stage 4 to Stage 5
Let Go of Spiritual Ego (Self-Centeredness)
Accept God's Purpose for Our Lives
Seek Wholeness through Personal Healing and Pilgrimage
Be Willing to Commit to Whatever It Takes

Crisis of Movement
Finding Peace through Giving Up the Search for Self
Allowing for New Certainty in God
Open to the Cost of Obedience

Question
Has your faith fallen apart? When? Why?

EXPERIENCING STAGE 4

QUESTIONS

1. What is your image of God?
2. How have you felt your image of God change from earlier times?
3. Has your faith fallen apart? When? Why?
4. Have you experienced a nagging search for personal meaning? How? When?

EXERCISES

Read the following stories. If they are part of your present journey, ask God to show you how you can identify with their forms of confusion, crises, or search for meaning.

- Peter's denial (Mark 14:66–72)
- Martha and Mary's confusion about the death of Lazarus and Jesus' power (John 11:20–37)
- Job's search for meaning in his suffering (Job 26–28)
- Elijah's story, when he has conquered the prophets of Baal, to Jezebel's displeasure, putting his life at stake (1 Kings 18:30–19:3)

7

The Wall

Although the Wall belongs clearly to stage 4, it is such a critical experience that we have chosen to discuss it in a separate chapter. Our wrestling with the Wall plays a vital role in the process of our spiritual healing. The Wall represents the place where another layer of transformation occurs and a renewed life of faith begins for those who feel called and have the courage to move into it.

The Wall represents our will meeting God's will face to face. We decide anew whether we are willing to surrender and let God direct our lives. Once we enter this part of stage 4, either through crisis, spiritual boredom, or a deep longing, we can easily become perplexed. Although we deeply desire to give our will over to God, and even believe we are doing so, in truth, we are trying to deal with the Wall in the same way we have gotten through life—on the strength of our own will or gifts. We try everything we can to scale it, circumvent it, burrow under it, leap over it, or simply ignore it. But the Wall remains!

What exactly is the Wall experience, and does everyone go through it? It is, of course, difficult to explain the Wall precisely since God is eminently personalized in stage 4. This experience is perhaps the most poignant example of mystery in the whole journey of faith. There is a deep sense of God at work in us in the Wall experience, and, at the same time, we are at a loss to describe it. We enter the Wall with fear and trepidation, but we become less afraid of being afraid because of God's leading. We are on holy ground. We are experiencing a pivotal moment when we feel drawn to surrender; knowing it will not be easy, but it will be worthwhile. We are dying to self and waiting to be reborn.

Our experience of God at the Wall takes on different nuances based on our personal needs for healing and renewal. Thus the Wall differs for everyone. Fundamentally, it has to do with slowly breaking through the barriers we have built between our will and a newer awareness of God in our lives. We have spent our own energy; we have come to the end of our ropes. We are ready to learn about freedom—the liberty of living without grasping. In a more profound sense than ever before, we have to "let God be God," and let God direct our lives. At the same time that we surrender our wills to be healed spiritually, we simultaneously begin to be healed psychologically. The Wall experience is the place where the two, psychology and spirituality, converge. Up to this point, one can be religious, spiritual, or fruitful *and* not be healed psychologically, or visa versa. The healing itself is mysterious and profound, for it is the soul that is healed.

Experiencing the Wall is both frightening and unpredictable. For some it requires a lengthy time. We have to take the thick Wall apart piece by piece. Others move through it rather quickly. Others will encounter the Wall repeatedly at different levels at different times.

Not everyone goes through the Wall. Some stop or get stuck at earlier stages in the journey and never get to the Wall. Others decide at the Wall to return to an earlier stage. Still others get stuck in front of the Wall, not wanting to submit to God.

TYPES OF RESISTANCE AT THE WALL

There are characteristic types of people who, when arriving at the Wall, try to avoid it or defeat it rather than experience it.

STRONG EGOS

Those of us in the first group think of ourselves as strong and talented. The struggle between God's will and our wills activates our feelings of self-sufficiency. We sincerely believe that we are in charge and, by being or doing good, can use our talents to control our own lives. It has worked that way for us for so long.

We try to scale the Wall, but we never reach the top. We frustrate ourselves by not recognizing that ultimately, if God is to be God in our lives, we cannot remain in control. For us, losing our ego-centeredness inevitably accompanies the journey *through* the Wall. And our egos resist vigorously. This experience, however, does not mean that we lose our self-esteem. Rather our ego-centeredness is changed to a God-centeredness by coming under God's control. A vast difference exists between humility and low self-esteem.

SELF-DEPRECATORS

At the other extreme, many of us encounter the Wall with self-deprecation. By putting ourselves down and not accepting God's free, deep, and enduring love, we continually try to measure up to unreal expectations. We never quite make it. We try to dig under the Wall only to learn that its foundations are much too deep. We miss the truth that in order to move *through* the Wall we must come to a deep and significant sense of God's uncondi-tional love and acceptance of us just as we are. Accepting God's love means accepting and realizing that we do have a self.

GUILT/SHAME-RIDDEN

Another group of us finds that the Wall represents painful and unwelcome memories. Frequently, these memories are found in devastating, guilt-ridden, or shameful events connected with the organized Church or with our family in our early years. Horror stories of being raised Catholic, Lutheran, Baptist (you name it) abound. Incest and abuse experiences are not unusual to dis-cover in our families—even "Christian" families. The memories now provide excuses for rejecting a God who had nothing to do with how the Church or the family misinterpreted God's love.

With this background we tend to want a spirituality or a deeper meaning but are unaware of the depth of the pain of our earlier experiences. We tend to substitute other forms of spiritu-ality for God in pursuit of something more comfortable for us. Consequently we dance in front of the Wall, exploring all our substitutes for God: for example, self-actualization, psychic experiences, New Age philosophy, positive thinking, human perfection, good physical condition, right living, peace projects, and moral codes. In the end, these substitutes represent the deification of humanity or the struggle to perfect our humanness. Rather, the Wall experience for us must manifest God's love and acceptance of us *in* our humanness. Tolerance of self and tolerance of others will be a major healing for us in this search. Paradox is the key. What is true is also false; that is, our church or family represented God but did not represent God. Our journey must make us see the other side of ourselves, of God, and of others. Going *through* the Wall means facing the ghosts in our memories and redeeming them by rediscovering God.

INTELLECTUALS

Of course, there will be intellectuals at the Wall. We try to rationalize and analyze it away. We think so much that we assume the Wall thinks too and can reason with us. We see it all as a game that we can win by outwitting our will or the Wall's. We have little interest in climbing, digging, or even in dancing. We will reason our way through. In fact, we doubt whether there really is a Wall. For us, going *through* the Wall requires a major softening, a loss of intellectual arrogance, and an acceptance of ambiguity and humility. For us it will be a humbling, at times a belittling, experience. We must learn to accept God's will without feeling the strain of wanting to debate it. We must learn to be vessels to be filled by God rather than by our own intelligence.

HIGH ACHIEVERS

We who are high achievers think we can build a higher wall and use it to jump over the Wall. We build it quickly and effectively. We work very hard and exert effort far beyond what is expected. Alas, our plan falters. We can never see the top of the Wall no matter how tall a Wall or vantage point we build. We too must go *through* the Wall.

Yet going through the Wall does not come as a result of our efforts. We can take no credit, nor can we be healed quickly or efficiently. We must simply let it happen. We must learn patience with the process of the Wall. It will not be like anything we have experienced before. We will be perplexed by the whole process. We will feel "reigned in" and unable to move at all for periods of time. But we will experience a peace and calm that we have never known before. The independent self will become an illusion to us.

DOCTRINAIRE

For the more doctrinaire, liberal or conservative, of us the Wall represents profound doubt about what we "knew" to be true. We deal with the Wall by drilling holes in it and attempting to weaken it enough to topple it. Paradoxically, we are drilling holes in our own perspectives too. Sooner or later our doctrines or knowledge will fail us. Our meeting the Wall will repeal our sense of security in right thinking. We must learn to rest in the mystery of ambiguity and intuitive guidance from God. Our security will come from our path to God and the experience of acceptance from God. Our journey *through* the Wall invites us to see another's point of view and to transform our own personal viewpoint.

ORDAINED

The ordained leaders of spiritual or religious groups among us have much at stake in holding to our groups' beliefs and causes, since we embody them for our followers. We sometimes approach the Wall by claiming spiritual power to destroy it and thus be vindicated in our role. We demand the Wall to crumble. We stand waiting for the Wall to respond obediently to our cry. Because we are deemed close to God, we feel God should respond to our requests. Substituting our own will for God's has become our weakness. How painful for us to realize that we, the leaders of the flock, also have to go *through* the Wall. We must come to terms with ourselves and face to face with God, no matter how differently God emerges in comparison to our expectations and teachings. This comes as a very humbling experience. It is difficult for spiritual leaders to become that vulnerable and face it. Spiritual pride is difficult to face, especially when in a position to lead others.

GOING THROUGH THE WALL

The process of meeting the Wall requires going through the Wall, not underneath it, over it, around it, or blasting it. We must go through it brick by brick, feeling and healing each element of our wills as we surrender to God's will. Our ego and will are transformed and made new. They are not transcended or risen above. We do not learn to get rid of them but to submit them. Along with spiritual healing comes psychological healing. We believe these transformations occur simultaneously at the Wall. We move toward wholeness and holiness. We do not get rid of ego or will. We release them. We let them be turned inside out so that unconditional love can emerge.

An example of the spiritual/psychological healing and transformation that occurs is the realization that fixing others, overhelping others, codependency, or excessive enabling of others is not selfless service. These motivations have unhealthy roots. They betray a sense of low self-esteem, a desire to control. Surrounded by God's love, we can work through the pain of these motivations toward healthy self-awareness and acceptance. That cloak of love allows us to accept our inadequacies while allowing God's grace to help us change or avoid situations that make us vulnerable. We do not become perfect. Rather, we rely on God to help us *care* about (not *take* care of *or* care for) others. We are more aware than ever of our own vulnerability. Only then can we evolve into more selfless service.

Doubtless it is apparent by now that we cannot go through the Wall by ourselves. We need God to lead us; otherwise our will would be in charge. Even approaching the Wall is uncomfortable because we feel both a pending loss and a great longing for new life, healing, or meaning. We bring anticipation and dread. We often experience grief at the Wall. Relief is the experience of others. Frequently, we also need a human guide to instruct, support, keep us on track, or just experience the Wall with us. This could be in the form of the written word and spiritual exercises, or it could be a person directing us through the Wall. The latter may be a friend who understands the experience, a minister, a trained spiritual director who knows how to keep us oriented toward God on our journey, or perhaps a wise psychological counselor who believes in the spiritual dimension to emotional healing. For some of us, just the act of putting ourselves in someone else's hands is a beginning of moving through the Wall experience. Accepting care and love from someone else is an important part of the process.

The experience of going through the Wall has led to some general lines of agreement about it. Not everyone experiences all of them. Some may have additional experiences. Mystery lies at the core of the Wall, a mystery that ultimately defies explanation but includes discomfort, surrender, healing, awareness, forgiveness, acceptance, love, closeness to God, discernment, melting, molding, and solitude and reflection.

DISCOMFORT

Some call it "the dark night of the soul," a time of feeling withered and alone, searching and not finding, or grieving and feeling a loss. Sometimes we feel so alone we think God has left us. Sitting alone in dark ambiguity is the result. These oppressive feelings and experiences are initially very much a part of the Wall.

SURRENDER

Something is always given up. That differs for each person. It usually is something central to one's identity. Giving up does not mean losing. It does mean release and detachment in whatever form that takes. There may be a prior sense of being unable to cope, of not knowing what to do or where to turn. Finally, in desperation we give up and let God do whatever is right for us.

HEALING

It is impossible to get through the Wall without recognizing past and present parts of us in need of psychological and spiritual healing and transformation. God does the healing as we sit humbly before the Presence and obediently follow God's agenda, an agenda that may not make sense to our common sense. At this time a personal guide may be very valuable to help us see the bigger picture and to hold our hands even when we cannot see where we are heading.

AWARENESS, FORGIVENESS, ACCEPTANCE, LOVE

There seems to be a four-phase movement—in one's self and toward others. It begins with an awareness of our shadow sides and hidden parts. These frequently are those things we see in other people that we do not like. It means being aware of all the lies we have accepted about ourselves and our families and all the myths of life that never were true. It means finding out who we are as opposed to who the world wants us to be. Although this may have occurred all through our life, it seems to be a major focus in the Wall experience. Frequently anger, bitterness, and sadness are part of this awareness process. All are necessary in order to experience forgiveness.

Forgiveness is the second phase. It means forgiving ourselves and others. Sometimes forgiveness is just a soaking process. It means fully absorbing the fact that we are different persons with stories different than we had thought. It can also be a real struggle, since we want to change things and make them look or feel better. We experience God's grace in forgiveness as we feel a sense of God's love for us, especially in our humanness.

The acceptance phase does not come easily for us. It goes a step further than forgiveness. We embrace ourselves. Acceptance means looking at ourselves in a detached way and celebrating the full range of our humanness. It means embracing the clown, the devil, the frightened child, the wicked witch, the lonely lover, the intellectual snob, the overachiever, the arrogant elitist, the insecure boy or girl, the outlandish dresser, the attention-seeker, the fool, the risk-taker, the addicted one, the beauty queen, or the perfectionist. If we do not embrace these parts, they will dominate us. By denying them, they become gods to us and control us. Ultimately they lead to suicide, just as do drugs and alcohol. By embracing them we mean to listen to what these qualities are telling us about ourselves. Usually they are messengers. For instance, a rising feeling of arrogance in a situation is frequently a symptom of insecurity. Knowing that, whenever arrogance arises, the deeper issue can surface, leading to acceptance. Fortunately, God constantly intervenes to help us by modeling forgiveness and acceptance. We must continually and humbly ask God for these gifts of forgiveness and acceptance.

The last phase of the movement comes with the emergence of love: love for ourselves, for God, and for others. This love, rooted in the awareness, forgiveness, and acceptance of ourselves, differs profoundly from what we have known before. We can love everyone, not just those whom we choose to love. We honestly care about others and their best interest and begin to see their needs above our own, not out of low self-esteem but out of overflowing love. Here we come face to face again with God, with God's love that heals our lives, calms our egos, soothes our chaotic wills into submission, and lets God direct our lives. And that moves us into the next stage of the journey.

CLOSENESS TO GOD

We experience God in a new and different way as we move through the Wall. Even when we feel God is absent, we sense that we are being kept on the journey. We sense that we are in process, especially if we are being guided by another at this point on the journey. In the previous stages, we believed intensely in God or in our "God" substitute. We felt very connected as long as things were under control or made sense. But now we find ourselves naked, defenseless, and vulnerable so that we sense God's love and presence in a new way. There is more of us available to feel, to be real, to let go, and to let show. At the same time, we can be more overwhelmed by God's pervasiveness.

DISCERNMENT

The Wall invites us to consider anything that God brings before us and to be open to understanding when it is of God. In a word, that means discernment. It means we suspend judgment, knowing, analyzing, or reverting to the tried and true—the good, old way. It may mean learning that all the good we thought we were doing was really a form of diversion from what God wants us to do or be. It means taking a risk and really listening to God in new ways, perhaps seeing God now as Provider, Healer, Friend, or Parent. It means letting go of rules, dogma, definitions, rational arguments, or whatever was our light and strength before. It means taking risks with people we love and people we do not love. It asks us to defer our judgment and let God lead, even when the results are ambiguous. Standing on hallowed ground, we find our foundations shaken.

MELTING, MOLDING

The hymn, "Spirit of the Living God," appropriately describes the Wall. It describes the moments of melting down and reshaping. "Spirit of the Living God, fall afresh on me. Melt me, mold me, fill me, use me. Spirit of the Living God, fall afresh on me." The melting and molding with fire and wax are excellent analogies of the Wall experience. Before the filling and using comes the time of melting and molding. Previously, we may have allowed God to melt an arm or leg, head or foot but now we offer more of our body, mind, and soul for melting and molding. Our soul pants for the Lord and waits in awe and expectation for God's presence. Longingly, the ancient Israelites sang this same prayer as recorded in Ps. 42:1–2.

SOLITUDE AND REFLECTION

We simply cannot go through the Wall while working sixty hours a week, whether at home, or in an office, or on the road. We must set aside time for solitude—time to walk, to listen to God's voice, to think, to feel, and to reflect. This, too, is highly individual, since one person's way of experiencing God differs from another's. But racing around defending our busy lifestyle is definitely not a way to solicit God's help. It simply means that we are not ready yet.

EXAMPLE OF A SPIRITUAL
JOURNEY AT THE WALL

Janet: As I reflect on my faith journey, it seems clear that I've spent more time in stages 2 and 4 than any of the others. I tend to be very intellectually curious, willing to explore, and sometimes compelled to search for my faith as in stage 4. And I tend to do this with at least a few other people who become my sense of community. I've not always been associated with the organized church, but I've almost always had some sense of community so important in stage 2. I realize now how much I need that.

The major times I've lived at stage 4 were during my ten-year agnostic and searching period and now during my intense period of spiritual direction and counseling. I think currently I'm experiencing stage 4 in a different way—exploring more of my core and moving in and out of the Wall.

During my ten-year agnostic and searching period I explored every possible alternative to my childhood faith. I was deeply immersed in psychology, which gave a lot of insight into human nature and maturation. I took seriously the admonition to "know thyself" in order to better help others. I also explored psychic phenomena, self-actualization theories and experiences, Eastern meditation and some Eastern religious practices, and the positive-thinking New Age philosophies. I learned many useful things about myself and many basic life principles that I still appreciate today. It was a rich and exciting time. I felt I'd found in these principles a way to express my spirituality that would not have to include my childhood memories and experiences, which were painful and made me angry. I didn't exactly hate the church, or I didn't think so then. I just thought it was irrelevant to my search. Meditation replaced prayer; positive thinking and good living replaced conscience. I could be strong, successful, spiritual, and self-actualized. When I was divorced, I realized that all these practices were useful but none of them was enough. Each one seemed to answer a question I wasn't asking. I was searching for the right question. I was stuck at stage 4. Finally I stopped and asked myself why I was doing all these things. My direction came in the form of another question that I'm still sitting with: "Who am I and who is God?"

The way I'm currently experiencing stage 4, The Journey Inward and the Wall, is through spiritual direction and counseling. In spiritual direction, quieting and coming face to face with

God are most of the process. Old concepts like prayer are integral to the journey, but they take on new forms and meanings. I describe prayer now as listening to God or experiencing God's presence. Sometimes it's simply life itself. Discipline is expected and eventually welcomed. Prayer and reading Scripture are part of the discipline. But Scripture reading is not zooming through the books of the Bible and memorizing verses. Instead I enter into verses and stories so completely that I'm there. I am the person being healed, asking questions, experiencing miracles, etc. I may stay with one verse for months before its fullness seeps deeply into me. Spiritual direction is more a way of life, a process of constant, further surrender of my will and my way to God's will.

Through spiritual direction I have found out why I was so wounded by my early religious experiences. I'm being healed. I can return to the early concepts, ideas, words, and images with appreciation, having experienced them now in a new way. I can see better how people misunderstood and mistakenly taught me, and I'm learning to forgive. It has been difficult, slow, and at times painful but worth the work.

Through counseling I have begun healing the family wounds of my childhood that have kept me stuck in my spiritual search. Spiritual direction provided me with the assurance that God would guide me through the counseling and that there would always be support. I was given the courage to embrace counseling. I'm learning to not be afraid of being afraid. It is difficult to face lingering wounds, pains, and fearful memories, but it is part of the journey. It is one experience of the Wall.

How have I changed? It's perhaps easier to ask others who have known me. Inside I feel calmer, more willing to listen to God and wait, more aware of my shadow side, less driven or goal-oriented, more forgiving when I'm disappointed with myself, more willing to laugh and play, more aware of what I like about myself and others, and more willing to love and be loved.

I feel like I'm just beginning to be unraveled, that I'll enter the Wall experience again and again at other levels. I'm excited and afraid to find out all the other new things that are likely to emerge in my life. But I pray I'll be ready and willing.

David: I feel so heavy, both physically and emotionally. Oh, I'm able to move about and relate to others, but I feel as though my spirit is poisoned.

For as long as I can remember, two important things were expected of me: to manage my own life and to serve others. I've succeeded at both and, at the same time, failed, since the result I really sought was to be loved. That rarely happened. Most of my life has been spent in academic or church circles with earned degrees and many years of experience for both. I believed that I had a ministry in both, so I gave of myself. Yet those people and institutions gladly used and then rejected me. *C'est la vie.*

Daily I struggle with bitterness and questions about life's purpose and life after life. Wishful thinking and self-pity constantly clamor within me as I strive to get a clear understanding of myself, of God, and of the link between us. I had been taught that the link was people. I no longer believe that.

My journey of life and faith is private and painful. I do not assume or wish it so for others. My goal is peace and joy, as the old gospel chorus says, "down in my heart." Yet part of my anguish seems to come because I'm seeking *my* dreams and *my* goals. The result is that I feel broken and vulnerable. More than I care to admit, tears regularly well up within me without warning. The message seems to be that I must abandon my dreams for the plans that God has for my life, even if I don't fully understand them. These are easy words to mouth but so very difficult for me to act on. This is an issue of faith.

It also appears to be a trap. It seems to me that, for educated persons in an industrialized society, our intellectual defenses and material allegiances are too well developed for us to be able to just let go and let the dynamic Spirit of God cleanse and renew us from within. We have not been conditioned to a simplicity of heart. Even the doctrinal and productivity aspects of institutional religion have encrusted my soul and encumbered my spiritual searching. There's that heaviness again; this time externally imposed.

I feel so alone on this journey and without worth. This is

further aggravated by my ongoing, long-term unemployment. Is it wrong to say that I am gifted in special ways worthy of employment? Is it wrong to be proud of my abilities and accomplishments? Or is that the sin of pride and therefore a stumbling block? I feel stymied. Yet I cling to the beliefs that a purposeful use of my skills is needed somewhere and that joy and peace are available (I'm learning not to say "attainable") if I can persevere, listen, and respond more openly to God's clues and cues. Does this require a guide?

Maybe I'm not broken enough yet; as horrible as that thought may be, I can't seem to move on under my own power. The constant questions are "How, God?" and "When, God?" The waiting for answers—for God's timing—adds to the heaviness. Clearly, I can't blame my impasse on insensitive people or institutions. I'm on the mat alone with God. No wonder Jacob's hip was dislocated. No wonder the frustration in Job's words: "I cry out to you, O God, but you do not answer; I stand up but you merely look at me." Is my charge to stop struggling and lamenting and simply to be obedient?

This is also an issue of will. And the very real outcome for me is heaven or hell right now. The extraordinary wisdom is that only as I choose to forego my will-o'-the-wisp ambitions will I gain for eternity that which I truly need but can't now grasp. It's another one of those paradoxes which wearies me. I'm tempted to shout, "But what's wrong with wanting to aspire, to be appreciated, to have peace and joy?"

Intellectually, I understand that the result is worth the risk. In reality, however, it seems too overwhelming to risk the precious little self-worth that I can claim. Total brokenness seems inevitable. "Please, Dear God, don't mock my struggles and don't drop me. Let me feel just a little of your presence and your love!"

EMERGING FROM THE WALL

The Wall experience is a necessary prerequisite to stage 5, the Journey Outward. Different ways of being will be asked of us at stage 5. We have to be able to distinguish spiritual truths from our own needs. We may be asked to give up important things, ideas, people, work, or parts of self for God's sake. Before the Wall experience, we would have interpreted these things as suffering. At stage 5 these sacrifices are no longer losses because we are aware of and more capable of understanding the nonsacrificial part of our selves. God's will is that our self-esteem be fully used in God's service. It ceases to be a sacrifice. Yet stage 5 is sacrificial. This paradox is difficult to explain simply because it is indeed a paradox.

So the mystery of the Wall remains a mystery. We sit in awe of the process of surrendering and going through the Wall. But, as we emerge, we are able to move along on our journeys with much less clarity about the direction and much more assurance of not having to be in charge of our lives. We are being transformed, turned inside out.

SUMMARY OF THE WALL

The mystery of our will meeting God's will face to face.

Types of Resistance at the Wall

Strong Egos

Self-Deprecators

Guilt/Shame-Ridden

Intellectuals

High Achievers

Doctrinaire

Ordained

Going through the Wall

Discomfort

Surrender

Healing

Awareness, Forgiveness, Acceptance, Love

Closeness to God

Discernment

Melting, Molding

Solitude and Reflection

Experiencing the Wall

QUESTIONS

1. Which is *your* best way to avoid the Wall?
2. How would your life be different if you could be healed from your deepest pains?
3. How have you experienced the Wall?

EXERCISES

Pick one or more of the following Scripture stories of Wall experiences and ask that God let it resonate in your life, if you are ready.

- Jonah while he was in the belly of the fish (Jon. 2:1–10)
- The woman with the twelve-year illness (Mark 5:25–34)
- Job in his desperate illness (Job 29–30)
- Elijah in his cave experience (1 Kings 19:4–14)
- Sarah, being barren and offering her maid to Abraham (Gen. 16:1–2)
- Mary Magdalene, before Jesus healed her (Luke 8:1–2)
- The women, when they first discover the empty tomb (Luke 23:55–24:5)

Talk over your experience with someone trained to help you sort it through.

8

Stage 5:
The Journey
Outward

"I've had a startling reawakening. For years I thought I knew what my real life purpose was. I thought I was doing it well, with God's help. Oh, was I misinformed. God had something else in mind, which my ego was not particularly interested in. Now my purpose is God's purpose for me and through me. My ego is quieting in reverence."

"I can't drive myself or get up for achievements the way I used to. Now I feel like God's child, to be used by him. Every day is a surprise."

"I am a servant to others because I love them. Whatever is asked of me I will do. God's love propels me to be there, to be available for others. That's all there is. That's life."

"I crave my time alone with the Spirit now. Before, I put in my daily prayer time and occasionally scrimped on God. Now I miss it deeply if I don't have that time. I look forward to how it changes my day."

"God has given me a life of love. I have peace more of the time. I am happy. Even with my physical pain I feel peace. No need to be rid of it or even to get better. It reminds me of my constant need for God."

"Fill me, use me."

"I know myself; I accept myself; I forgive myself; I love myself because God does."

"I am weak, unable to do anything on my own. Only through the grace of God am I able to function."

"God's grace and love are sufficient."

Stage 5, the Journey Outward, is the next step after rediscovering God and accepting love. Now we surrender to God's will to fully direct our lives, but with our eyes wide open, aware but unafraid of the consequences. Once parts of the deep, excruciating inward journey have been experienced, the natural outcome is to venture outside of one's self-centeredness and back into the active world with a new sense of fulfillment. This is the outward journey, a venture outside our self-interests to others, based on the growth and peace of mind we have experienced from the inner journey. This outward venture may or may not be different from our previous direction, but our focus is different. Our focus is outward, but from a new, grounded center of ourselves. Once again, we have been changed. We have experienced new wholeness. We are aware of our faults and have a fresh desire to be in God's will rather than our own. We know we are surrendering to a much wiser, more vital Spirit. We sense a looser grip on ourselves and a willingness to be conduits for God's work in our lives and others' lives. We endure suffering gracefully, because our confidence is in God.

Our primary motivation in life becomes the desire to love honestly and live according to God's purposes. Consequently, for some, life patterns, work habits, friends, and ways of being may slowly change, although that is certainly not an automatic result of the stage 5 experience. We feel at times weak, vital, humble, patient, obedient, loving, and willing—words we might not have used earlier to describe ourselves. As our interior patterns change, we may be confused. Yet this is a time for waiting on the Lord to renew our strength instead of a time for long-range planning.

How do you talk about what is going on at this stage in the journey? That becomes one of the dilemmas. The healing and calling experiences are so personal and profound that they are difficult to express. When we do verbalize our faith at this stage, we often use the same language, analogies, and images used at stages 1 and 2. Yet the language does not convey the surrender, the experience of our own painful path to healing and wholeness in God, or our real sense of call. So at stage 5 we do not try to explain our experience or distinguish it from previous experiences. We have little interest in being recognized unless someone inquires of us personally. We simply do not concentrate on ourselves.

How do you recognize people at this stage? This too presents a dilemma. We are at times difficult to distinguish because we are not eager to be distinguished. It also is easy to confuse people at this stage with those at stage 2, since both are surrendering in different ways. In stage 2, we surrender to that life of which we are sure. In stage 5, we surrender to that life purpose which we have yet to know or understand. At stage 5 we at times may be very vulnerable and unclear about our lives and direction, but there is an inner peace and calmness about us that is mystifying. We know that in this very lack of clarity, God is showing us our call.

CHARACTERISTICS OF STAGE 5

A RENEWED SENSE OF GOD'S ACCEPTANCE

There is a human tendency to think that if God really knew us God would not love us. At stage 4 we meet ourselves, discover forgiveness, and experience healing. Yet the healing process and integration must continue. At stage 5 we grow into the full awareness that God truly loves us even though we are never fully whole. God loves us in our humanness. Therein lies a deep, divine humor. Consequently, we can really laugh at ourselves and not feel put down, but loved. This sense of humor is so unique that it bears further explanation.

At this stage we experience a humor, cosmic and divine, that causes us to chuckle at things that may not have seemed funny before. Humor is not at the expense of others but related to ourselves and to small coincidences. For instance, we rush late to a meeting, forgetting to turn it over to God, only to find the other members late as well. Or we chuckle over the way in which a cat gives orders to its owners, or the way we receive humorous puns in dreams. It is a gentle, soothing, warming humor. We gain a renewed sense of God's unconditional love for us as seen both in the ultimate and continuing sacrifices God makes on our behalf. God never leaves us. It is we who leave God. At this stage we recognize and accept the responsibility for the times we leave God. We feel fully loved and accepted by God and become ready to do God's will in our lives instead of substituting our own egos for God's will.

We realize life is not living to our "fullest potential" but living far beyond what we thought our potential was, perhaps even using skills we did not know we had or did not even like. Patience, for instance, frequently arises at this stage for people who never had it or prided themselves in getting things accomplished efficiently. Charles Schultz, in his comic strip "Peanuts," has Lucy say to Charlie Brown, after emerging with disgust from prayer, "I was praying for patience and understanding, but I quit. I was afraid I might get it." Lucy's human nature is so like our own.

Wholeness looks a lot like weakness at this stage. Wholeness does not make us stronger; it allows God to work through our weaknesses. Wholeness means being very aware of our faults but not letting them trip us. Wholeness does not mean we are in charge; it allows us to wait for God to direct. Wholeness does not make us complicated; it helps us discover our simplicity. God can use us most in our brokenness, a truth that was very hard to accept until the Wall experience.

One of the great Bible stories illustrates not only this characteristic of stage 5 but almost all characteristics of this stage. It is the story of Hannah, the mother of Samuel, found in 1 Samuel 1–2. Hannah, one of two wives of Elkanah, had no children. This gave her an inferior status in a culture where children, especially male children, were considered to be a blessing from God and a measure of one's status. Her social standing in the family became painfully clear at thanksgiving season when the other wife would mock her for not having had any children.

Out of desperation one year, she poured out her heart to God, pleading for a child. To her delight God responded, and she conceived a son. Now she had what had been missing in her life. She was blessed by God. But instead of keeping the child for herself, as soon as he was weaned, Hannah gave the lad to God and to the service of the Temple. She knew that, ultimately, he was God's child, the answer to her prayers. So Samuel grew up to become one of the great prophets in Israel, the one to anoint Israel's first king, King Saul, and later to discover Israel's ideal king, King David.

However, despite Hannah's grateful gesture of giving back to God what God had granted to her, she never ceased being Samuel's mother. Each year she would take a new robe that she had made for her son when they went as a family to make their annual pilgrimage to the holy place (1 Sam. 2:19).

A NEW SENSE OF THE HORIZONTAL LIFE

In stage 4, The Journey Inward, the focus was on the vertical relationship between us and God. We needed to go inside and do a lot of talking, battling, crying, listening, defending, and surrendering to make our relationship right with God. That may even have meant healing from our previous images of God or God substitutes. The emphasis was narrow, intense, and vigorous. At stage 5 the ponderous work of the most intense healing lies behind us. We continue to be healed and come more alive in various ways throughout life, but the concentrated darkness is over for now. The movement at stage 5 is on the horizontal, the outward, the reaching out to other people from a sense of fullness, of being loved by God, and being asked to love others in return. It is such a natural process that we hardly recognize it happening. Our hearts are different, and our lives evolve from that change. As we said before, people at this stage may even be surprised at the talents, skills, or qualities they have been given in order to be horizontal people—qualities that they did not know they had. Led to move horizontally, they discover that they are equipped to do so.

Living horizontally means becoming aware that God's

purpose for our inner lives is lived out in the world, whether for "the many" (larger causes) or for "the one" (serving one or two people). God may ask us to live out our true inner purpose differently from what we had supposed. We come to realize that God's purpose corresponds with our own deep longing and purpose that we were not yet aware of. It was there all along. We were just too busy, too noisy, or too successful to see it. When we see it, we begin to live into it with our whole selves—not by ourselves, but more dependent on God and with more confidence in God. This development sometimes requires our giving up something we were clinging to, like our idea of work, our rigorous approach to physical fitness, our hold on our children, or our intellectual cynicism. This too is part of the journey.

In Isa. 42:1–4, we have a song to an anonymous servant who illustrates this kind of living. Called by God and equipped by God's Spirit, the servant moves outward to right the wrongs of his world (42:1, "he will bring forth justice to the nations"). Yet he does so without fanfare (42:2, "He will not cry or lift up his voice, or make it heard in the street") and with gentleness (42:3, "a bruised reed he will not break, and a dimly burning wick he will not quench"). He persists despite clear opposition.

SENSE OF CALLING, VOCATION, OR MINISTRY

Along with the distinct move to the horizontal comes a somewhat disturbing or relieving call from God either to be different in our life's work or to be in a different life's work. If we have made major ego investments in our work, whether raising a family, running a department, or hitting golf balls, we may well be asked to transform either our approach to our work or the work itself. If, for instance, love becomes the central factor in our life, then the way we talk, give feedback, argue, direct, console, encourage may have to change. If our work has been so all-consuming that we cannot slowly disengage in a healthy way, we may have to disengage completely. This does not mean that coming into stage 5 demands a career change, but it does mean a slow transformation in the way we go about our life's work.

At this stage we begin to experience God's choices for us as our calling. We are not in charge. We do not do the planning. We feel compelled by God to live differently, to work differently, to obey our call. We long for God, for the sense of oneness with love. We may be surprised by what God asks for or calls us to do because it may be small, humble, risky or new, but we are willing because we are trusting God to provide the means, including even the financial means. We are sometimes surprised at how simple or mundane our life's call is, yet how profound it becomes. For instance, a life purpose of being available hardly sounds exciting. Yet it can and does open us to new experiences that were unknown before. When we experience *all* we have and are as gifts from God, then we can be "poor" and more dependent on God.

The calling comes from God at this stage, not from another person (guru, spiritual leader, friend, teacher) who interprets God's call for us. That is part of our discernment process—how to hear God's call and distinguish it from other calls. Others may hear God's call for themselves but cannot hear God's call for us. At this stage of the journey, we can generally distinguish our own wishes from God's wishes because of our discipline of communication through prayer, the Scriptures, and daily quiet reflection with God to discern the Spirit.

Perhaps no story is more touching than the story of Mary's call to give birth to Jesus. Singled out and informed to her surprise of the coming pregnancy, she queried only to learn that it was to be of God. She willing responded to the call that would totally disrupt her life with "I am the handmaid of the Lord; let it be to me according to your word" (Luke 1:38).

CONCERN AND FOCUS ON OTHERS'
BEST INTERESTS

At stage 5, winning, losing, accomplishing tasks are secondary to us. The focus is more on process, not getting there, and on our role with others. Our major concern is not ourselves. We are aware of maintaining a healthy self-image and not excluding self, but the subtle shift in focus is from ourselves to others and then to the world. This focus does not arise out of a need to take care of others, to change others, to fix others, to live through others, or even to negate ourselves or be martyrs. Rather, it comes out of a fullness of God's love for us and for them. It could mean a nurturing that stretches us beyond our comprehension. It could mean just being there and doing the right thing—the thing God asks us to do.

At this stage we will sacrifice for others by going out of our way to help them, heal them, listen to them, live with them, or hold their hands. This can occur in our own backyards and also around the world. We feel that we are part of a larger humanity whom God loves and wants us to serve. We get in the trenches with people as well as stand on top of the mountain cheering. We are willing even to suffer with others. We join with people all along the way because we want to and because God asks us to be there. Even if we lose something as a result, we persevere. We will risk misunderstanding, ridicule, danger, and even pain to do what we are called to do. However simple or difficult each step seems, we take it with the assurance that the step is right because God is leading. So it does not seem like sacrifice or suffering in the way it would have earlier. We have our times of doubt, but we bring these doubts to God as well, for we are dependent on God.

When we employ stage 5 behavior, we occasionally baffle others with our quiet, behind-the-scenes type of behavior. For example, we can do things that are considered by most beyond the call of duty, but we don't feel that way about them at all. Examples might be: despite a busy schedule taking a neighbor to her weekly physical treatments for three years, or supporting a nonrelative through college, or offering to listen after hours to employees who don't work for us anymore, or taking in an orphaned child. This behavior is beyond duty, done out of love, and compelled from a fullness and wholeness. It's miraculous but real.

We do not burn out at this stage. We know ourselves well enough to avoid, or if necessary to tolerate, emotionally draining situations or job settings. We are given insight and grace by God to keep ourselves continually aware of our emotional and physical health and limits. We have learned how to go about our calling with a patience and freshness, a vitality that can only come from God. Living in and through the Spirit of God, we serve others out of love. We can even love beyond our own constraints, because God is at work enabling and activating us. For instance, without bearing a grudge, we can work with or serve people who in the past have hurt us or cheated us.

Look at the story of Joseph in Genesis 36–50. His entire life seemed full of people trying to destroy him. Yet, in one instance after the other, he not only survived the various attempts at ruining him, but he had more than one occasion to take revenge on his enemies. Each time, however, Joseph sought only to do what was in the others' best interests. His confidence in God's grace shines through his memorable words to his brothers: "You meant evil against me; but God meant it for good" (50:20).

A DEEP CALM OR STILLNESS

"Be Still My Soul" is a strong theme at stage 5. There is a new longing just to be simply in the presence of God's fullness. Frequently during the day, thoughts of God pervade us. We can be serene, joyful, alive, and unafraid again. We have our special times of listening, praying, seeing, and being with God. We feel the light of God flooding through us, taking away fear. We can go through loss, pain, joy, sorrow, grief, or happiness without so frequently losing touch with God.

At this point in the journey, we let God be God from the inside out instead of the outside in. We let God direct our lives from a calm stillness inside, from a peace of soul and mind. We can be ourselves fully as fragile, spotty, incomplete, and imperfect, yet wise, loved, willing and called. It is a miracle to be able to let ourselves be used fully by God despite our shortcomings. In fact, God even fully uses our shortcomings. All are gifts to us.

At this stage we often feel a longing to be quiet inside, to be still, to listen and wait, even when we are busy in the world. We carry a calmness or stillness with us that permeates the room and touches others without fanfare. We often have a quiet, peaceful quality that draws others toward us as a companion or friend. We can be direct and honest and, at the same time, loving and caring. We move with the Spirit on a day-by-day basis, being available to whomever God has put in our path that day. We can be vulnerable and feel safe because we know we are loved.

We know about loving others. Out of our quietness comes a deep understanding and wisdom that sustains our horizontal journey. In fact, our inner stillness, coming from peace with God, is the source for our outward journey. When we get out of sorts or out of touch with God, we may lose our calmness for a time. Then our personal journey is to move back into relationship with God. In fact, most of our journey at this point is to stay in close touch with God. We may even say, "Lord, I've lost you and am not even capable of knowing how to approach you. Help me to come back." Despite our awareness of God and our life of prayer empowered by the Spirit, we know that we too can get out of touch. We are even more aware of our fragility and need for constant companionship with God. We know personally how vulnerable love can be.

Daniel in the lions' den illustrates the kind of calm that comes in the face of even great danger when one has a sense of God's calling and purpose. In Daniel 6 it is recorded that King Darius was tricked by his advisers into getting Daniel arrested and cast to the lions. To his chagrin, the king followed through with his edict only to spend a restless night worrying about Daniel's fate. His rush to the den in the early morning was met by Daniel's reply, "O king, live for ever! My God sent his angel and shut the lions' mouths, and they have not hurt me" (Dan. 6:21–22). His calm contrasted vividly with the king's anxieties.

EXAMPLE OF A SPIRITUAL JOURNEY AT STAGE 5

Verne: How does one speak of his travel on the journey of faith? Perhaps by analogy. Most of us have enjoyed a vacation from which we returned refreshed and satisfied. For some a single experience has been so satisfying that we could even say, on reflection, the trip would have been worthwhile even if we had memories only of that one event. But rarely, in our fast-paced living does anyone stop and recognize while still on the journey how pleasing and nourishing the experience is at the time.

Rather, we package and photograph the moments, consult our schedules, and rush on to the next item on the agenda, confident that we can recapture the joy at a later day. If you are one of the lucky ones who can remember a time in the midst of travel when you stopped long enough to say "thank you, God, for having me here," then you will understand a little of my journey of faith.

It is the sense of present completeness that I wanted to use as the analogy, not the easy-going, worry-free life of a vacationer.

I am thankful for today and the privilege of all the yesterdays that have been mine. I have lived already for more years than my father. I have known the love of a wife, the nurture of a mother, the respect of my children, the regard of my colleagues, and the pleasure of many friendships. And I have the assurance that I am known to God.

Today, I do not set goals of accomplishment, rather of relationships. I am at home in the world of goals and productivity and time lines. Yet, they are not mine. I will work with them to honor you and ultimately God, for I sense that my role is to serve.

Regrets and ambitions? Alas, yes. Still for neither would I ask your sympathy. For the moment I feel quite at home in the hand of God. Given the grace of time, I will do more, see more, and have added regrets. I am not ready to retire, but I am prepared for this to be the last day.

My desire is that you know the God who has known me. That you find support and be support within your circle of family and friends that I have shared with mine.

Ruth: During the Lenten season of my first year in parish ministry, I reached a point of near burnout. It became clear to me that it was important to get away for a few days after Easter to sort out some things concerning my future in ministry. I called a local retreat center and reserved space for a four-day, private retreat beginning the day after Easter. I didn't know it then, but that quiet time would have a profound impact on the future course of my professional ministry.

Feeling tired, frustrated, and confused, I began on the first day of that retreat to ask myself the difficult questions. Am I cut out for ministry in Christ's church after all? Is it too demanding for me physically, emotionally, even spiritually? The answer to both these questions, for me, was yes. But then, by the grace of God, came a more important question for me to consider. Is the way I have been doing ministry the past several months the only way to do ministry? That for me, became the focus of my reflection for the next several days, and slowly I came to know in that time of retreat that the fast-paced, program-filled, eighty-hour workweek of the large suburban parish was not the only way, certainly not the best way, for me to do ministry.

I craved balance in my life. Time for doing, but also time for being. Time for action, but time, too, for retreat. That dimension of quiet, that sense of balance had been missing in my ministry throughout the course of that year. I went home refreshed and with a new sense of vision for myself and for the parish ministry.

For the next four years I tried to make it work. Bringing balance into my own spiritual life was relatively easy. It meant saying no to some things. It meant being diligent about daily times of quiet or prayer and meditation. It meant monthly retreat days away. I was intentional about seeking balance in my own life, and, in time, I worked out a daily and weekly routine that worked for me.

Bringing balance into the life of that busy parish proved to be much more difficult, particularly in the light of the fact that as an associate pastor I had to answer to someone else. Staff demands and occasionally the demands of the parishioners in that large church seemed to be never ending. When I said no, it often created a sense of tension and guilt inside me, and I felt constantly at odds with some significant assumptions operating in that setting. At the same time I felt a growing sense of frustration over the fact that there never seemed to be time to grow deeper with people. There were always new programs and fresh challenges, leaving little time to savor and reflect.

In time I came to realize that it was time for me to move out of the parish ministry and into a specialized ministry of spiritual renewal. In my heart I longed for the parish to be different. I wanted it to be a place that encouraged people to slow down and seek balance in their own lives. My wish was that it could model for people in our fast-paced society a better and deeper and truer way to live out the claims of the gospel. But I felt like a "voice crying in the wilderness," and I knew it was important to my own spiritual journey to move out and find other, and for me, more effective ways to minister.

I miss the sense of ongoing community in the parish setting. I miss some of the aspects of ministry I am not as often involved in now. But I treasure the constant opportunities I now have to journey deeper with people in one-to-one and in small group relationships. My own journey of faith has been greatly enriched by this work. Perhaps some day I will be called to work with a people of vision to create a new model for parish ministry. For now it is important for me to work outside and in partnership with the model that exists.

CAGED AT STAGE 5

The description of the cage at stage 5 differs considerably from the previous stages. In fact, we do not really become caged or stuck at stages five and six. We have become healed (willing to love all of ourselves, the shadow and the light) and are living in the fullness of God's purpose for our lives. We can certainly regress and become stuck at an earlier stage. But it is virtually impossible to become stuck at stage 5.

This does not mean that we do not appear to be stuck to others. We most certainly do. Our behavior can be very frustrating to those at other stages—especially to those at stages 2 and 3. Just being at stage 5 looks very stuck to them. This results from some of the characteristics of this stage.

SEEMINGLY OUT OF TOUCH WITH PRACTICAL CONCERNS

Frequently, we appear to be impractical and out of touch with reality. The way the world functions around us, people who are other directed, whole, selfless, and called by God are counterculture. When we love people despite their having failed miserably in our society for whatever reason, we are called naive; when we stay with the grieving, we are considered caretakers; when we give money away, we are considered poor managers; when we yield, we are considered noncompetitive; when we let go, we are considered weak. We just do not fit with the realistic expectations of a world that is out to be productive and to win. Even the productive Christians at earlier stages in the journey think we at stage 5 have lost our edge.

It is difficult to explain to people that being impractical and unrealistic is at times the right thing to be. Yet at this stage we care neither for recognition nor to be understood. We are aware of being seen as unrealistic, but we have an immense compassion for others that allows us to be tolerant and loving even of others who view us adversely. We do not need to change them or be seen as holier than others. To the contrary, we frequently agree that we are impractical and then quietly continue with what we are doing for God and others. Our focus is not on the prize but on God who is love.

At stage 5 we are not as oriented toward productivity with outward signs or products. Consequently, we appear less productive and slightly isolated. We are in fact quite active. But we have a tendency to do things behind the scenes or on a one-to-one basis. We never realize that we are hardly noticed. This style can be very confusing and even frustrating for those who want us to be leaders in the more traditional way.

APPARENTLY CARELESS ABOUT "IMPORTANT" THINGS

To many, we appear not only uninvolved in the critical faith and Church/community issues but almost unconcerned about them. We appear not even to care about the really important things such as creeds, rules, controversies, new directions, new theories, new members, education, raising money, musical programs, holiday festivals, or saving souls. You name it. We will most likely not be at the center of it. Instead, we will often be behind the scenes doing whatever we are truly called to do. And when doing what we know we are called to do does put us at center stage, we are there in a more detached way. We have a genuine sense of wholeness in God.

MOVING FROM STAGE 5 TO 6

NO STRIVING, JUST EVOLVING

This transition is barely discernible from the outside. From the inside it feels like there is just more of God and less of us. Our craving for God increases, as we seem to decrease. And paradoxically, the less we know about or care about this transition, the more likely it is to happen. For the focus is not on us anymore. The focus is on God and others, with total dependence being the key.

The evolution creeps in and invades the soul. Eventually we feel the striving cease, and we are not sure when it happened. The issue is how and when we can sacrifice our entire lives to God. The opportunity is just out of reach, but it will be there, and it will be compelling. And it seems so right and emerges out of such a healed heart that there is no longer any doubt in our minds. We are beginning to experience what it means to be sons and daughters of God.

SEEING GOD IN ALL OF LIFE

The movement to stage 6 is exemplified most by the still, small voice, the whispering that comes to us from everyday, life experiences. The major difference from before is that all things, events, people, illnesses, joys, successes, and life changes "smack" of God. We have a close, personal awareness of God in all things. Any grasping, even spiritual grasping, ceases and the life of love begins to evolve. We provide no direction or control. Everything begins to simplify and love simply shines through.

BEING GOD'S PERSON

This life of love furthers a process that has already begun. It means developing into a more adequate representation of myself, the person God created me to be. It means being Christ-like in the way Christ was fully himself. I own my weaknesses and let them become an occasion for my strengths ("When I am weak, then I am strong" [2 Cor. 12:10]). I discover that God uses all of me as a whole, healed person to touch other people, even when I am unaware of the connection. I begin to see myself as an instrument, a gift, an extension cord for God. This also means understanding how to get out of God's way. I live love: tough love, blind love, forgiving love, self-love. In short, unconditional love.

CRISIS OF MOVEMENT FROM
STAGE 5 TO STAGE 6

"VOCATION" IS SATISFYING

To some of us it has taken so long to know what calling or work we are to do and how we are to be in that calling that we justifiably relish our newfound calm and consistency. We are content to know that God is working through us and that we are in God's hands. We get energy from the Source and feel renewed and satisfied, like you would after a savory, but not too filling, meal. We just want to continue doing our calling and not be called to another level of commitment now.

BEING WHOLE SEEMS ENOUGH

For many of us the struggle and pain of the journey through stage 4 and the Wall, along with the subsequent revisiting of the Wall, has been a monumental venture, one that we imagined would take us all of our lives. Now we can see that, by constantly being open to God's healing, we can slowly evolve to more wholeness. That discovery when we never believed it to be true before, is so powerful and awesome, that we think it is all we can expect to experience in our lifetimes. And for that we are grateful.

What we fail to see, unless we once again lean into the unknown, is that there is more love to come. And it is the most enduring love of all, sacrificial love.

SUMMARY OF STAGE 5:
THE JOURNEY OUTWARD
Thesis: Faith is surrendering to God.

Characteristics
A Renewed Sense of God's Acceptance
A New Sense of the Horizontal Life
Sense of Calling, Vocation, or Ministry
Concern and Focus on Others' Best Interests
A Deep Calm or Stillness

Caged at Stage 5
Seemingly Out of Touch with Practical Concerns
Apparently Careless about "Important" Things

Moving from Stage 5 to Stage 6
No Striving, Just Evolving—Growing Deeper
Seeing God in All of Life
Being God's Person

Crisis of Movement
"Vocation" Is Satisfying
Being Whole Seems Enough

Question
Do you have a glimpse of God's purpose for your life?

EXPERIENCING STAGE 5

QUESTIONS

1. When have you been given more energy or stamina than you had to survive a crisis, illness, growth time (and not experienced burnout)?
2. When have you been "given" the right words or qualities to be available for another?
3. Do you have a glimpse of *God's* purpose (vocation, call, ministry) for your life?
4. How are you experiencing the shift from vertical to horizontal living?

EXERCISES

Pick one or more of the following Scripture stories of people surrendering to a life calling after a Wall experience. Ask God to let you experience this transition, if this is the time for you to be called.

- Hannah receiving God's gift of Samuel and giving him over to God (1 Sam. 1:1–28)
- Jonah changing direction from Tarshish to Nineveh where he dreaded going (Jon. 3:1–5)
- Mary, when she finds out how and who she will conceive (Luke 1:26–38, 46–55—The Magnificat)
- Job listening to God and being reconciled with God (Job 40–42:6)
- Joseph forgiving his brothers after they had sold him into slavery in Egypt and he became ruler of Egypt (Gen. 45:1–15)
- Isaiah and Jeremiah allowing their lives to be changed by God to become prophets (Jer. 2:5–9; Isa. 6:1–8)

9

Stage 6:
The Life of Love

"This is God's trip. I'm just a passenger."

"God is love and that's all that matters."

"Others are my purpose."

"Obeying God is my purpose, new every day."

"Take my life."

Stage 6, The Life of Love, is easily summarized. At this stage we reflect God to others in the world more clearly and consistently than we ever thought possible. We let our lights shine in such a way that God is given the credit and the thanks. In many ways, at this stage we represent an extension of stage 5. Yet the characteristics of stage 5 are more complete, just as stage 3 represents a more confident, fuller version of stage 2.

When we are at stage 6, we have lost ourselves in the equation, and at the same time we have truly found ourselves. We are selfless. This factor allows us to do the most extraordinary things. We may figuratively wash other people's feet or give our very lives in the service of God (at times that means we die to self; at times it has meant and can mean that we die literally). We are at peace with ourselves, fully conscious of being the person God has created us to be. Obedience comes very naturally without deliberation because we are so immersed in God's work, wherever that may be such as in the field, the school, the home, the corporation, the prison, or the neighborhood. We give our all without feeling that it means surrender or sacrifice. We are at one in the Spirit with God, who is our head and heart. Sometimes people at stage 3 are confused with those at stage 6. Both are eager to expend themselves and be obedient to God. The people at stage 3, however, give to God what they can afford to give of time, talents, possessions, and money. People at stage 6 give more than they can afford; in fact, they give all they have without any sense that giving is in any way a sacrifice.

Even though it may be very difficult for others to understand us at this stage, people can be uplifted in spirit just by being with us, whether in joys or hardships. We can live openly and vulnerably with others, because we do not need self protection. Consequently, at this stage we are involved intimately in the lives of others to whom God calls us. In constant dialogue with God, our lives are permeated with unconditional love.

CHARACTERISTICS OF STAGE 6

CHRIST-LIKE LIVING IN TOTAL
OBEDIENCE TO GOD

At this stage, Christ's life represents not just an example but a model for our lives. We willingly are obedient to God's call, even, if necessary, unto death. We have wisdom that God gives to direct and sustain us. We begin to understand deeply the paradoxes and pains of Christ's life.

Our times alone with God come during the quiet times away as well as in the everyday, unceasing conversations. We have little ambition for being well known, rich, successful, noteworthy, goal-oriented, or "spiritual." We are like vessels into which God pours his Spirit, constantly overflowing. We are Spirit-filled but in a quiet, unassuming way. So pervasive is the presence of the Spirit in our lives that we may not even be particularly conscious of doing something of the Spirit. We are oblivious to the Spirit because we are accustomed to God moving very naturally through our lives, unexpectedly and surely. Consequently, we are genuinely humble and able to talk of our lives and purposes in very simple terms.

WISDOM GAINED FROM LIFE'S STRUGGLES

When at stage 6 we still experience pain or shock, it tires or angers us, but we can also simultaneously experience God's grace, humor, and comfort in the midst of it all. We do not fear pain, trauma, disappointments, or even death, because God is there to provide and to lead us on. For us life's struggles provide a source of wisdom, a source for further learning, and a means to new discovery. We are aware that miracles can occur more frequently through pain than through joy. We experience life itself as both a gift and as a miracle.

Many times we feel personally small, insignificant, or unsuited to the task God has for us. But God promises to use our weakness to do God's work. We can respond in ways that utterly astound others, because we are not operating on our own power or energy anymore. We are God's. That is enough. It does not matter what we do, where we live, how we look, or what we eat. We totally believe that God cares for us as much as for the birds of the air and the lilies of the field.

Although many see Jesus as operating with a special advantage of knowing everything, and thus knowing the end from the beginning, the Jesus of the Gospels goes through his own growth and development. He saw his way prefigured in the Hebrew Scriptures as the suffering servant rather than as a conquering hero. He learned from his rejection by the religious authorities, his friends, and his family. He was not surprised by the disloyalty of his own disciples. On the night before his death, Jesus prayed for God to provide another way, but only if it was God's will, which he was committed to follow.

COMPASSIONATE LIVING FOR OTHERS

At stage 6 we can reach far beyond our own capacity and love our fellow human beings with deep compassion, because we know that all come from and are loved by God. As Jesus was compassionate even in Gethsemane, at his trial, and on the cross, so we are compassionate under extreme hardship. We can live and work with people we never imagined we would even want to have contact with. In Gandhi's autobiography, he told a practicing Muslim that if he truly wanted forgiveness and love to flow from God, he should raise the child of a Hindu man who had murdered the questioner's son in his home. Not only that, but, most difficult of all, he should raise the child as a Hindu. The man looked shocked and walked away. A stage 6 person could raise an enemy's child because of the compassion given him or her by God. Yet compassion does not mean to be lacking convictions or the absence of anger. It means that, in the midst of anger, we are still willing to love, help, and be there for others.

We can certainly serve and live with people we like at stage 6. We also can immerse ourselves in the lives of people who may have hurt, repulsed, or even been repugnant to us. We do this out of God's overflowing love in us, rather than as a challenge.

Jesus models this kind of life by reflecting compassion for the poor, the hungry, the sick, and the possessed. Rejected by his closest friends, he repeatedly accepts them in their disillusionment. The victim of torture, executed by the barbaric act of crucifixion, dying in the midday sun with the taunts of the surrounding crowd, Jesus prays for their forgiveness. He even extends the healing touch to untouchables like the lepers and the dead. He "came not to be served but to serve, and to give his life as a ransom for many" (Mark 10:45).

DETACHMENT FROM THINGS AND STRESS

At stage 6 we become aware that the more of God we have, the less of everything else we need. We do not renounce material possessions. We simply learn to need them less; we become detached from things and people as props or bolstering devices. We emerge from inside ourselves with a glow that does not need to be enhanced. We may not even be in good health, nor do we need to be beautiful by the world's standards, but we are wonderful by God's standards. We gracefully accept life and have an inner satisfaction no matter how little we have outwardly. In fact, we really do not think about how much or how little we have.

It is not that we do not appreciate nice things, beauty, health, and happiness. We do. But we are not attached to nice things or to things in general. We are free of encumbrances. We travel light.

Jesus' itinerant style of life reflected his detachment from earthly possessions. Often seen as the guest in a home or at dinner, he had learned that God's call to him meant freedom from things and stress. When a man asked him what he needed to do to know life, Jesus told him to sell his possessions, give the proceeds to the poor, and become one of his disciples (Mark 10:21). When another sought to follow him, Jesus reminded the young man that "Foxes have holes, and birds of the air have nests; but the Son of Man has nowhere to lay his head" (Matt. 8:20). Yet we never find Jesus anywhere in the Gospels fretting over food, clothing or shelter. Rather, we hear him in the Sermon on the Mount exhorting his disciples to "seek first [God's] kingdom, and his righteousness" instead of worrying about food, drink, clothing, or what's coming tomorrow (Matt. 6:25, 33).

LIFE UNDERNEATH OR ON TOP

We choose to do anything God asks, whether the most menial or the most prestigious things. We can be close to God either way. In the giving up of our wills at stage 5 we now actually delight in doing the menial. It gives us great joy and raises our spirits to a new level. We soar with eagles when we are about the most mundane tasks, because God has blessed us with love. For us to empty a bedpan with love can be the highest calling to which we can respond. It's up to God. Or we can, against our own common sense, become a central figure in a cause or mission. Whatever we do, it is clear that it is not of our own doing.

We are full of surprises because we are so free, so full of God, and so whole. We can say or do preposterous things because we are not afraid of death. We can deliberately give up our lives, materially, physically, mentally, and emotionally for the service of others without feeling afraid of the deep loss. We are selfless, so who we are does not matter. What matters is who God is and who God makes us.

We have no greater illustration of this characteristic than in the story of Jesus' taking a towel at the Last Supper and washing the feet of each of his twelve disciples. The task of washing feet belonged to the household servant. Jesus did this as an act of love and concern for his friends (John 13:4–10).

LIFE ABANDONED

We seem to disregard our own needs and not care for ourselves at this stage. This is because those needs are secondary to our need to totally obey God and listen for God's direction. So we can even give up our lives for a person, a cause, or a principle if it is God's will. Other people consider this a high sacrifice and most difficult to comprehend—especially because it does not seem like a sacrifice to us at this stage.

But in our example, others can sense that God is very much at work and that many will be affected because of the way that we lived. It has been said that, on the night before he died, one of the great Christian saints had a strange sense that it would happen. He didn't change his plans, but he did send his wife flowers for no apparent reason. Perhaps, in that instant, he knew what it meant to be obedient to God.

When Pilate threatened Jesus with his power and vowed to have him crucified, Jesus responded that Pilate was helpless to do anything unless power from above had been given to him (John 19:11). The early Christian hymn in Phil. 2:6–11 notes how Jesus went humbly and obediently to death on the cross. His surrender of his life is portrayed graphically in the words of Luke 23:46: "Father, into thy hands I commit my spirit."

CAGED AT STAGE 6: THE LIFE OF LOVE

SEPARATION FROM THE WORLD

As with stage 5, we are not really caged at stage 6, but appear so to others. At stage 6 we look totally out of touch with the real world. We appear unappreciative of the critical things of life. We have a God-given ability to give up anything for the sake of our faith: family, friends, security, money, work positions, or life itself. Though an irony for us, such "giving up" does not seem like a sacrifice. We seldom reflect on it. It was simply something we had to do. We do not do it for selfish or self-serving reasons. We are so in tune with God, so at one with God's will, that our motives are God's motives. We are simply living love. And that confuses others.

NEGLECT OF SELF

Sometimes we appear to neglect ourselves because we are not concerned with the things of self. Our joy is in having God live in and through us. We frequently are simple in life, simple in speech, simple in possessions, simple in friendship and family, and simple in faith. And it is so hard for our world to understand simplicity.

APPARENT WASTE OF LIFE

We even appear to give up or waste our lives unnecessarily. Our work could be done differently. For example, consider a person who felt called by God to live with and minister to AIDS patients in the inner city. That seems frightening and so unnecessary when giving money, or volunteering once a month, or praying for them would also help. In Camus's book, *The Plague*, there is a doctor who stayed with plague victims rather than leave them unattended. He knew that his chances of contracting the disease would be extremely high. He did it anyway. He found life's meaning in giving up his life for his "friends."

At this stage we offer others a true test, since our lives belie so many of their expectations. But when we begin to uncover more of what it means to let go and let God be God, our behavior becomes clear and profound in its simplicity. Truly we live the life of love.

SUMMARY OF STAGE 6:
THE LIFE OF LOVE
Thesis: Faith is reflecting God.

Characteristics
Christ-like Living in Total Obedience to God
Wisdom Gained from Life's Struggles
Compassionate Living for Others
Detachment from Things and Stress
Life Underneath or on Top
Life Abandoned

Caged at Stage 6
Separation from the World
Neglect of Self
Apparent Waste of Life

Question
How is God everything to you?

EXPERIENCING STAGE 6

QUESTIONS

1. How is God everything for you?

2. How do you feel called to sacrifice yourself for others with no attachments?

3. How are you detached from self and the world and attached to God?

EXERCISE

Read the life of Christ in one of the Gospels and ask God to lead you into that kind of surrender if this is the time for you.

Postscript

Now that we have described our model of the stages of faith, we want to remind you about what is fundamental to the journey: The critical journey is a process driven by the dynamic of God and our wills. While both of us appreciate and need conceptual models, we also agree that they can mask the process described. In fact, models can be mistaken for the process itself. The faith journey is especially vulnerable to that error. By concentrating on the model more than the process, the traveler can miss, at least for the moment, the fact that "God moves in mysterious ways his wonders to perform."

As we continue to move in our own faith journeys, we have been reminded of the dynamic nature of the various stages. Both of us have moved forward and backward to different stages during the writing of this book. We have noticed especially when we have approached the Wall or moved into it for a time that we are drawn back to earlier stages where we find rest or the beginning of growth in a new area of our faith.

For instance, Bob has undergone open-heart surgery as we neared the completion of this manuscript and felt very much a

161

part of stages 1 and 2 again. On the one hand, he felt the over-whelming awe and gratitude for being in God's care and know-ing the healing that comes from God. He again was aware of how powerless he was and how much his life was in God's hands. In the fall of 1988 he also moved from the church setting back into a seminary setting. During the period of major transition, he was unable to say with certainty where he was on the model. Transi-tions tend to obscure the end results. Yet he has had a clear sense of peace and direction that God was in the move.

Janet, on the other hand, has spent what she considers to be an inordinate amount of time in the Wall. She has observed the rearrangement of her own life. Now she is apprenticing once again (stage 2) for a different way of working. While still work-ing in the corporate world, her message there is changing. And she has more one-to-one meetings, especially around issues of spirituality! She has entered a training program to become a spiritual director working in a secular setting. Her work with women from prison occupies a special place in her life. And she is more convinced that life itself is an adventure.

So we urge you, as we continue to remind ourselves, to seek the high road, to yield to God, and not to limit God's ways to any human paradigm. In the long run it is perhaps best to know about the stages and then not fret about them. Rather just let God be God in your lives. That is the stuff of the critical journey!